P9-DGQ-065

I Second *That* Emotion

I Second *That* Emotion

Untangling Our Zany Feelings

Patsy Clairmont

THOMAS NELSON
Since 1798

NASHVILLE DALLAS MEXICO CITY RIO DE JANEIRO BEIJING

Published in Nashville, Tennessee, by Thomas Nelson. Thomas Nelson is a registered trademark of Thomas Nelson, Inc.

Thomas Nelson, Inc., titles may be purchased in bulk for educational, business, fund-raising, or sales promotional use. For information, please e-mail SpecialMarkets@ThomasNelson.com.

Library of Congress Cataloging-in-Publication Data

Clairmont, Patsy.
I second that emotion : untangling our zany feelings / Patsy Clairmont.
p. cm.
ISBN 0-8499-1949-5
1. Christian women—Religious life. 2. Emotions—Religious aspects—Christianity.
I. Title.
BV4527.C5329 2008
248.4—dc22 2007049733

Printed in the United States of America
08 09 10 11 12 13 QW 9 8 7 6 5

To Carol Porter,

whose fifty-year friendship

has been one of

God's sweetest gifts

to my life

Contents

Introduction

Contain Yourself

Hey, who supersized my emotions? I don't remember ordering an extra large wad of rubber-band emotions at the take-out window of life, but, honey, I've got 'em! No wonder I sometimes snarl and snap at folks; it's all those elastic knots inside me.

This isn't a new condition for me, but menopause hasn't exactly enhanced the situation. Instead, it has added, ahem, emotional dynamics that my family claims I didn't need. I took that as a compliment.

I thought by the time a woman reached my age, she pretty much had her emotions cinched in. Don't get me wrong, I've improved. Honest. Les, my husband of forty-five years, is still alive, and that's proof I'm doing better (just kidding . . . sorta). The poor guy has had his hands full, dealing in the past with my radical reactions and now my hot-flashing hormones.

I have come to understand that life is constantly pressing our buttons because people, circumstances, changes, hormonal shifts, and our emotions (his too) combine to make us works in progress.

I hope that's a relief for you to hear. You aren't the only one who at times feels that you have more mood swings than brain cells and more hormones than hallelujahs. Nor are you the only one who is married to a man with a set of reactive emotions. I've raised one husband and two sons, and I promise you that men have emotional cycles too.

Emotions aren't an indictment against our spirituality but rather proof of our humanity. Whew!

So take a deep breath and pour a cup of green tea. No, wait, go ahead and pop a dark chocolate bonbon. We girls are in this together. And there's nothing like girlfriend gab to help us feel that we aren't weird but, instead, are intricately woven together with fine golden filaments . . . Okay, would you believe with a surplus of colored rubber bands? But what's a person supposed to do with all these elasticized ribbons?

Well, Les and I paid our first visit to the Container Store recently. At this stage of life we call a visit to a new store a "date." We hold hands and walk down the aisles saying, "Oh, look at that . . . Ooh . . . Ah." I know, I know, that really douses the sizzle in romance.

Anyway, I noticed the employees were wearing T-shirts emblazoned with the words "Contain Yourself." It made me giggle.

We saw every kind of container to provide us a custom place to stash our stuff. Les and I left an hour later with big grins and enough containers to organize a flea market.

But the T-shirts kept coming back to my mind: "Contain Yourself." What a great idea for our zany emotions, but how does one do that without imploding? Chances are, even the most calm and relaxed among us will, before our tour of duty is done down here on earth, pop her cork, spewing rubber bands hither and yon, because humanity is hard to keep under wraps.

I guess we could try to cram our irritations in under-bed storage containers, or jam our crankiness into hatboxes and shove them to the backs of our closets, or toss our bad attitudes into hampers and nail the tops shut. But, alas, we can't. I know; I tried.

What we can do is to recognize that our little rubber-band fits can provide clues in our quest to unravel our emotions. Snappy answers, sarcasm, overreactions, passive-aggressive behavior, pouting, outbursts, and cynicism are some of anger's containers.

We often think our anger is someone else's fault. Why, if he hadn't done what he did, if she hadn't said what she said . . . yada, yada, yada. That approach is as old as Eden and doesn't hold apple juice.

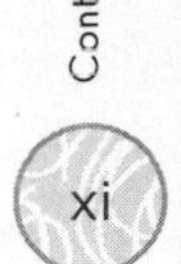

And I, Ms. Dribble Cup herself, should know since anger has been both my habitual covert and overt hiding place. After living with the havoc my anger created relationally and internally, I was forced to seek alternative ways to handle my inner upheaval. Most importantly, I learned anger is about us . . . we might be overtaxed, we may not be feeling well, or possibly someone has said or done something that snaps an old rubber band from our past. We may not even be aware that our strong response isn't so much about today but, instead, showcases our yesterday and another person or situation. Something similar in the circumstance has tightened a knot and—bam!—we react.

Recently that happened to me. A friend, whom we'll call Gilda, made a comment that sent me into an emotional tailspin. The statement wasn't mean or unkind, but nonetheless a tangle of painful feelings swelled up in me.

After a while I had a little chat with me. It went something like this:

"Honey-girl, that reaction is way too big for the comment. You need to get a grip. What are you feeling?"

"Like I've done something wrong, but I don't know what it is. I feel shamed."

"When in the past did you feel like this?"

"When I was a child," came my immediate answer to myself.

"Who made you feel that way?"

I instantly knew.

I'm not suggesting we should be our own full-time therapists, but sometimes we can fill the bill. I ended up in a split-personality conversation because I couldn't stop obsessing about the exchange between Gilda and me until I examined where all those rubber-band feelings originated. Once I looked at it objectively and answered the questions honestly, the mulling stopped.

We're wonderfully made, I know, but, boy, we surely are emotionally intricate.

A number of years ago I brought to a speaking engagement a bulging wad of rubber bands that I had knotted together to show women how I often feel emotionally. I had no idea how many others felt the same way until I pulled that colorful mass out of my bag and heard the roar and applause of the gals in attendance. Let's face it: we gals are filthy rich emotionally, which can be taxing.

In the chapters ahead we'll pull some of our stretchy emotions out to examine them individually. This won't be an exhaustive look at our feelings, but instead think of it more like a rubber-band spa—a place to be refreshed, revived, and maybe even repaired a little.

For the many years that God has generously allowed me a speaking platform, I have addressed two topics: women's emotions and the counsel of God's Word. I might approach those subjects from different angles and from different life seasons, but these are issues I'm passionate about. That's because I've been a cracked pot full of rubber-band emotions in need of divine counsel for as long as I can remember.

For many years my feelings dictated the quality of my life until Christ's intervention. While my efforts to contain myself have been gradual, change has continued, providing me with insights along the way—insights that I pray will hearten you and perhaps offer you some shortcuts so you don't have to make all the pit stops I did. And if you're in a pit stop, I know the well-used Map that helped me will help you as well.

When we combine life's circumstances with our emotions, they can add up to a tidal wave threatening to sweep us away. But we need to remind each other that we can talk to the One who speaks peace to the storm. We need to chat about some of the feelings that tie us in knots. And I'll share what we might do to take the next step in our untangling journey.

God's Word is full of helps for emotions like grief, moodiness, fearfulness, anger, self-pity, and other human responses. We don't want our negative emotions to rule our lives and thereby permeate the quality of our existence and relationships. If we're ruled by anger, we're likely to become dictatorial; fear, given full reign, will make us recluses; and loss, unchecked, will cause us to ooze bitterness.

As we go along, we'll giggle, because I've noted that laughter is the key to restoring perspective. Besides, humor rescues us from taking ourselves too seriously. There's nothing worse than a cranky old woman who can't see past her furrowed brow or a young woman who can't see past her own reflection.

A reporter was interviewing a 104-year-old woman and asked her, "So what's the best thing about being 104?"

She quipped, "No peer pressure."

Now, that makes me laugh aloud. May we all live to be 104 and still have our humor intact. That kind of spunk helps us to survive and thrive—survive hardships and thrive with a firm grip on joy.

Until then, let's wend our way through the dense tangle of emotions that make us tender and tough, sweet and surly, forgiving and frightful, calm and tense. We are a study in complexity. But guess what? God is up to the task. He wants us to be balanced and beautiful inside and out. His treatments last longer than Botox. And that's great news for an aging Tilt-O-Whirl like me.

I love the story about the woman who thought she was "lookin' so good" as she sashayed down Main Street, only to discover that last night's pantyhose were hanging out of her trousers for the world to see . . . oh, wait, that woman was *me*! Now, that kind of display, honey, will make you tense right up.

Yes, life exposes our weaknesses, but the good news is, we all have them. We have snarls of stretchy emotions and wads of dangling pantyhose. So this will be a book of emotional mutuality . . . no outcasts here.

Sharpen your pencil because in the back there is a workbook to help you personalize emotion-comforting truth, and a DVD of video clips from messages I've done through the years at Women of Faith conferences. Those ought to stir up some lively discussions as I toss my rubber bands around like a lasso in hopes of capturing your attention and helping you laugh truth into your innermost parts. Watch as I sit on a hot seat, take on an intruder, and become part of a Wild West show.

Come join me, and let's add some snap to our zany, emotion-filled lives!

1

Pierced Years

In the midst of winter, I finally learned there
was in me an invincible summer.

— Albert Camus —

If there's a season within me, as Albert Camus's quote suggests, I know my season would have to be a blustery one. It is my way to do too much and say too much. Quite honestly it's more natural for me to bluster about in a flurry of activity or talk up a full-fledged whirlwind than to "Be still and know . . ." I think that's because if I'm quiet too long and listen carefully to the still small voice within I will have to own my behavior and I will "know" I need to change. Change requires much, is scary, and is about as appealing to me as sushi. Trust me, I don't do raw. Yet I long to be . . . sweeter, deeper, kinder, and less aware of my deficiencies. Don't you?

It's not a mystery that we all at sometime or other feel like our hearts have a hole in them where our confidence regularly seeps out. Because of sin, no one escapes the "woe is me" syndrome. Gratefully in this chapter Good News is ahead.

We all are born kicking and screaming, demanding to be cuddled, comforted, and convinced that we are safe, that we are secure. Come to think of it, some grown-ups are still doing that. As little ones we go through predictable childish phases: we hold our breath, refuse to potty train, and demand constant attention. Yet even with society's latest child-rearing guides and our family's heroic efforts, we still grow up with fractures in our self-esteem. Our sense of self is pierced.

These insecurities are aggravated throughout our lives by events, people, words, misunderstandings, betrayals, losses, and our own frailties. Did I mention people? Let me say it again: people. Ah, that felt good. I mean, really, don't some folks just jitterbug all over your last nerve? They're so good at it that it makes one wonder if it's their gift.

Insecurity is in everyone's DNA ever since the apple scandal in Genesis that resulted in the garden's gates swinging closed tight. There went paradise . . . for now.

Speaking of paradise lost, where is your "garden" today? Not the one with silver bells and little maids all in a row, but the place, room, corner of your universe where you feel safe and secure . . . or at least a little *more* secure? I need spaces where I can read, pray, and write. Even if it's a designated chair or a porch swing, I need somewhere to go again and again to become still. Quiet reflection gives me a place to untie some of the knots, not only in my wad of rubber bands but also in my neck, back, and shoulders. And it gives me some time to recover from life's demands.

Today I have a couple of "hiding places." Oh, they're visible, but I've designated them in my own mind as my places of refuge with the Lord. One is a cozy reading chair with chubby arms (the chair's, not mine), poochie pillows (the chair's, not mine), and a reading lamp. Other times I convince Les he needs to go to Home Depot (a suggestion he relishes), and then I make the first floor of our home my walking, talking sanctuary. I pace from room to room talking aloud to the Lord. It's very helpful.

Besides having physical spots that I burrow into, I also have a place in my mind I can scamper to when the need arises. Years ago I was challenged to close my eyes and imagine a mental space where I could sit and talk to Jesus. I was told I could make it a garden, a seaside, a mountaintop, or anywhere that felt safe and private. I chose a living room with high-backed, overstuffed chairs in front of a fireplace, and nearby were open French doors that emptied onto a terrace filled with flowers. When I felt insecure, even if I wasn't home, I could close my eyes and go to that place to gain my bearings.

Okay, now you try it. Close your eyes and create a space, and then the next time you're trapped in, say, a checkout line, have a little mental tea with the Savior.

I confess, though, that I often sabotage my best intentions to be still and take care of my emotional self. Quite frankly, sometimes I'm the snake in my own garden. You wouldn't believe all the excuses I can hiss when I have a book deadline. Instead of writing, I feel compelled to single-handedly construct an addition onto my home, shingle my roof, or join a traveling clogging troop. Then, added to the urge to do something radical like dust, I feel my insecurities rise up within me.

I believe we can add to or subtract from our sense of worth by the choices we make. Isn't our insecurity all about a leak in the dam of our self-worth? Pause and think about it.

It's downright scary to be handed an accurate picture of ourselves, physical or verbal, yet those moments reveal who we are and how we feel about ourselves. And the revelations can help us finally nestle into Christ's acceptance.

I recently went to a doctor who specialized in skin. The darling, young, unwrinkled aesthetician looked at me and said, "Let's just be honest: have you considered a face lift?" I told her she would need to do a body lift if she wanted to straighten my many folds. Actually, I went in hoping for a good face cream that wouldn't cause my skin to break out, but she wanted to raze the building and start over. Bless her unblemished heart; she was fearless in her willingness to tackle any size project. We settled on a sun-blocking face cream.

Here's what's truly amazing: Christ loves us, double chins, smudged hearts, blemished minds, and all.

Have you ever looked at a photograph of yourself and asked someone, in an incredulous tone, "Do I really look like this?" Additionally stunning is the answer, as one such soul replied recently to me, "Pretty much."

It's not the way we had thought we looked or even wanted to because we're certain we appear, well, you know, cuter, thinner, and younger. Why, I've seen photos that made me look exceedingly, uh, antique. Imagine that! I'd like to think of that as trick photography, but as a friend quipped recently, "Yeah, the trick's on us."

Gloria, a friend of mine, attended her school reunion. A former classmate approached her and said, "Boy, you sure let yourself go." How rude was that? The caustic remark robbed Gloria of the event's joy, but it also lit a fire under her motivation. Somewhere deep inside her, instead of unraveling, she committed to losing the weight that gradually had increased over the years. Within seven months of hard work and discipline, she was the smallest she had been since her school days. Gloria looked smashing.

I don't applaud the rude former classmate, but I do celebrate my friend, who had the maturity and courage not to make that exchange about someone else's bad manners. Instead she looked at what was true, and then did something about it. It's easy, when we feel insulted, to indulge our insecurities by making comments about the other person's poor social skills.

See if you've ever said these things to yourself about a person who has been critical of you:

"She is just insensitive."

"He is so judgmental."

"She doesn't understand how hard I've tried."

"Besides, who is he to talk?"

While all that deflection may be accurate about our accusers, the important question is, "Is what they said true?" If it is, what are we willing to do to change?

Let's say we truly have tried to change. Then the question becomes, "Are we willing to try again?"

The dictionary defines *insecurity* three ways: 1. subject to fears and doubts; 2. not safe; 3. not firmly placed or fastened.

Being a former agoraphobic, I should have earned a degree in fear, because by the time I became housebound during my twenties, I had stockpiled an eighteen-wheeler full of knotted rubber bands. I could have started my own elastic company.

I worked hard to step into the freedom I experience today, but that doesn't mean I don't have moments when I am "subject to fears and doubts." For instance, my heart always beats faster before I step onto the stage in an arena in front of thousands of people. I think, *What if I fall? What if I forget what I wanted to say? What if the audience doesn't like me?*

What if . . . What if . . . What if . . .

We can drive ourselves bonkers with that kind of "insecurity kindling," which only keeps our insecurity sparking.

The truth be told, I've fallen onstage more than once (the last time it was in front of sixteen thousand people, I might add), and do you know what happened? I got up again.

My young friend Lori, new to speaking from a platform, recently fell on her way onto the stage, bounced back onto her feet, made the announcements, and sat down. After a moment she leaned over to the stage manager and asked, "Did I dream it, or did I just fall in front of an arena full of people?"

"Sorry, it wasn't a dream," the messenger whispered. And you know what Lori did? She marched back up on the stage over and over again all weekend and did so with dignity, grace, and humor.

I'm sorry to confess that I've forgotten what I wanted to say onstage more times than I want to admit. Do you know what happened? I just said something anyway.

And there have been times I've bombed, and do you know what happened? I forgave myself and tried again.

We are far more resilient than we realize. That's part of Albert Camus's "invincible summer" when he says, "In the midst of winter, I finally learned there was in me, an invincible summer."

We shouldn't be jarred during an emotional blast of winter to find that, when we experience an emotion, it's tied to other emotions. For instance, insecurity can be directly affected by shivering shame, which we will chat about in another chapter. So don't be surprised if you get two for the price of one during hard times. I've found that, when insecurity tugs on my shirttail, shame is close by.

At first glance shy people seem to have cornered the market on insecurity, but it just isn't so. Their reticent manner may give them away more quickly, but we all have a dandy case of insecurity.

I think the hardest people to help with insecurity are those who appear headstrong and capable. You can be highly visible, quite capable, even impressively successful, and yet feel deeply insecure.

Sometimes old messages die hard, and if you came out of, say, verbal abuse, working harder and achieving more aren't going to silence the voices. Nor is withholding yourself from public scrutiny. Because we are human, we usually go to extremes to shake off background chatter from our past, but that seldom brings resolution.

Verbal abuse has a long shelf life. I think we have all heard the worst forms of word slinging—perhaps in a grocery store, a relative's home, or even from a friend. But less obvious forms of verbal abuse can affect the hearer as well.

Twelve days after I turned twenty years old, I delivered my first child. As thrilling as that was, I was neither emotionally healthy nor mature enough to handle motherhood. I was full of fears, anger, shame, and insecurities.

Even though our desire is to give our children a rich heritage, we give them what we have and what we have known. They become the recipients of our best, though faulty, efforts.

After my firstborn became an adult, he confronted me about some hurtful words I had spoken to him as a child. He told me that I had often called him "stupid." I was stunned. *No way! I wouldn't do that. I don't talk that way, especially to a child.*

My husband jumped in to protect me, saying he never remembered my speaking that way. But our son wasn't being cruel, just honest. Honesty can feel crushing, but when faced, it can bring about emotional resolution. Hours later, as I thought back, I remembered that at times I did react inappropriately. When my son was doing something silly, I might say in frustration, "Don't be stupid," "Now that was stupid," or "What a stupid thing that was."

We talked about those old exchanges, and I pointed out that I never said my *son* was stupid but that what he was *doing* was troublesome to an inexperienced mommy. He agreed and then added, "All I heard was 'stupid.'" And that, my friend, is what matters—what he heard. Words cut deep trenches into young hearts.

I was so sad to think that I had hurt him and marred his self-esteem. I'm the mom, and I was supposed to protect my boy from others who might say mean things. My son forgave me, but forgiving myself took much longer.

My reactionary words to my dear son were about me, not him. Words are powerful and can feel indelible. And because we have so many words, before our days are done we will hurt others. I promise you that none of us, regardless of our desire or our discipline, will slip through this life without word regrets—what we shouldn't have said and what was never said that should have been spoken.

I encourage you to ask forgiveness of those you have slung words at, possibly bruising their sense of value. You can't erase what you said, but you can clear the static in your relationship. And if you've held back something that you know you should have uttered, run to them and say it.

Then you'll need to visit your "garden" for a talk with Jesus about the difficult task of forgiving yourself. If you're like me, you'll have to make repeated visits because I keep forgetting that forgiveness is a done deal.

We have every reason to be insecure, except that Jesus gave his life for us emotional ragamuffins. He came to give us a new self-concept based on his acceptance, which is vast. Christ sees us, knows us, and—get this—loves us.

So I invite Christ into my sitting room near the fireplace. The smell of lilacs wafts in from the terrace, and I see the last sparks playing in the fire that took the chill off the morning air. I tell Jesus of my failure, but he already knows. Before I can finish asking him to forgive me, I can tell he already has. I feel the dark smudges on my heart disappear.

Find your summer place. Talk to Jesus. He is the only invincible one who can rescue us from ourselves and heal us of our insecurities.

2

Nervous Nellie

Fear grows in the dark: if you think there's a bogeyman around, turn on the light.

—Dorothy Thompson

"Fear has friends," I warn women when I address the topic of being afraid. When you emotionally surrender to one fear, you open the door to a myriad of others. I learned that the hard way, through my own experience. And I paid with years of my life. I'd like to offer you a shortcut.

When I gave in to a fear, let's say the fear of riding in an airplane, then, sure as shootin', fear not only brought his suitcase and moved in, but he also had relatives tucked into his baggage. The next thing I knew I avoided elevators, then expressways, soon crowded rooms, and before long I was staying home with a houseful of scary "babysitters." That's how I grew up to be an agoraphobic . . . at least that's the condensed version.

I learned to protect my emotional well-being by setting boundaries on who and what enter my house (mind) and even my yard (imagination). I had to post No Trespassing signs, and on the bottom of the signs in bold letters I willed myself to write, *"And I mean it!"* This firm decision helped protect my mind and my imagination.

When we make up our minds to take our emotional health seriously, we will do whatever is necessary to take care of ourselves. That includes breaking the habit of indulging fear's fanatical need for attention. Fear, with its narcissistic mentality, clamors for attention. Trust me, we can't afford what that will cost us in liberty, self-respect, and mental health.

My recovery has been slow. At least emotionally it feels that way. My friend Marilyn Meberg has reminded me that "emotions don't have brains," so it's important that we not let them do our thinking. Yet Marilyn, a former therapist, would also tell us that to ignore our emotions is another extreme we can't afford. I don't know how you're wired, but I'm given to extremes. I have to be on guard that I don't swing into an abyss of my own making.

But rather than plunging us deep down, emotions can also bring us back up and tenderly connect us to others. They allow us to experience joy, wonder, and love. And they help us to evaluate how we're feeling about ourselves, others, and God. So emotions are vital if we're to enter the fullness of life that Christ offers. Yet emotions unchecked can leave us flighty, flaky, and full of fears.

Because fear ruled my life for years, I never expected I would one day travel back and forth across our nation speaking on stages before hundreds of thousands of women. And I surely didn't anticipate that I would have the thrill of traveling to other parts of the world, first to Israel and then Africa. Me? Israel? Africa? Wow! Even now, as I write this, I'm flabbergasted.

I was in Africa just two and a half months ago. It took nine flights and eleven days to make memories that will last a lifetime.

I could never have taken trips in my agoraphobic years, and quite honestly, I wouldn't have chosen to do international trips even several years ago because I wasn't certain I could handle the demands of such whirlwind jaunts. I never had a desire to be a globetrotter; besides, I didn't like the idea of being that far from my husband and family. So making the decision to go was, for me, a big deal and another step of facing the fear of the unknown and growing in my faith.

Faith is a journey I believe we never complete until we see the sweet feet of Jesus. That means, as long as we have breath in our bodies, we can learn more, do more, and see more. During my agoraphobic days, if I'd owned a pair of binoculars that could see into the future and I'd caught a gander of myself boarding an airplane to fly to Africa, I would have known I was watching a fantasy—and yet here I am today having lived the reality. Fear is such a tormentor determined to hem us in and keep us stuck. But Jesus our liberator is still opening prison doors to set his people free. I didn't dash out my door when it opened, I inched out with sweaty palms and thumping heart as I gradually learned to trust that, regardless of where I was, Christ was with me . . . even on the other side of the world.

I've come so far from the days when I couldn't even drive to the grocery store, yet I still have moments in which I feel hesitant to venture into uncharted territory. Trust me, traveling to other countries has the potential of putting stretch marks on my rubber bands.

Going so far to such a different land presented me with a number of mental obstacles I had to scale. First were the shots. I'm not afraid of needles, but because I tend to be drug sensitive, I can work myself into a dither anticipating a reaction. So I can't tell you what relief I felt to go with my Porch Pals (a nickname for the Women of Faith speakers who sit on a little porch while waiting for their turn to speak) to have the injections. There really is something about numbers that helps, especially when those people are full of faith and fun. They were a wonderfully wacky distraction.

When the nurse called my name to step in the next room for my first shot, Marilyn, Luci, and Sheila all stood up. The nurse wasn't as encouraged by their desire to be supportive as I was, but she did let someone go with me each time, and that was comforting. In two office visits we had a total of six or seven shots. I lost count after a while. My friends diverted me because they knew that fear is inflated or deflated by the mental time and attention we give it. I was too busy with my pals to comply with fear's obsessive needs.

I've found that, when I huff and puff fear, I can make it a runaway hot air balloon full of panic and wild imaginations. Or I can keep things in perspective, which initially takes a lot of self-talk. But then fear shrivels down and becomes a more manageable size.

Once the shots were in order, the next discomfort for me was flying over the ocean, which turned out to be a nonissue once we were off the ground. I wondered if all that water beneath us would bother me, but it didn't. That fear was quickly put to rest; of course, it helped that we had a smooth ride.

We had been warned not to drink the water or even brush our teeth with tap water while in Africa. We also were cautioned about our food choices, where we ate, and not to leave our hotel unaccompanied while in Nairobi. The list was detailed and could have become mental fodder for an ex-phobic. In fact, I could have worked myself into a dither if I hadn't maintained good thought boundaries. Add to that, when we arrived, I noted armed guards outside the hotel and for a moment wondered if FedEx could overnight me back to Michigan.

A few days later we flew out of Nairobi in a single-engine plane over the savannahs to the Masai Mara Lodge. Our bush pilot was young, which gave me pause. Actually any pilot on such a runt of a plane would have deepened my prayer life. I just wasn't sure I wanted to fly in such a tiny aircraft with only one engine. But again I was surprised that once I was onboard I enjoyed the flight. Even landing on a dirt path in the middle of nowhere was exciting.

What actually did scare me silly happened before we boarded. We had to step up on a large scale in front of our group and be weighed. *Carumba!* It's definitely knee-knocking to have one's most personal info plastered on a billboard-size screen. Okay, okay, so fear inflates reality, but the numbers were red, about three inches high, and could be seen by the naked eye at least to the Canary Islands. (And the canaries were shocked.)

Just so you get the picture of the petite aircraft we flew in, let me say our luggage had to be driven to the lodge because the airplane couldn't safely carry that much weight. Hello. After we were weighed, we were assigned seats to balance the aircraft according to the number that had rudely popped up.

I was praying nobody sneezed or even turned around lest we head for the earth prematurely. Actually, it turned out the only one who couldn't sit still during the flight was neck-craning me, because I was trying not to miss the spectacular landscape out the windows.

After arriving at the Masai Mara Lodge, we journeyed to a remote village where we were to visit a family that lived in the hills in a hut. I was looking forward to it even though the ride was hard and jostling.

The visit was touching, but part of the adventure of that day still lay before us—we just didn't know it. The ride back to our lodge, which should have taken three hours, took five. We were tossed and bounced every which way but out the window (only because it was closed).

Unbeknownst to us, while we had been village visiting, hard rains had fallen for miles around our lodge and had left the cratered roads in fragile condition. We were still miles from the lodge's safety, evening was falling, and we were seeing all kinds of wild, I repeat, *wild* animals on the savannah. Then we spotted an armed government official on the road ahead. As we neared, he flagged us down to chat with our driver. The driver was told he couldn't proceed on the roads, but we must instead travel on the water-soaked savannah.

As bad as the roads were, may I just say the savannah was much worse. To keep from sinking axle-deep the driver had to floor it. We all hung on as we careened up and down water-filled ruts and ditches. At one point I spotted, through the sprays of water off our tires, a hippo just a few feet away. My stress level rose, but to my surprise I was enjoying the raucous ride.

Then it happened. Just ahead of us was a herd of water buffalo. Now, if you haven't been up close and personal with a water buffalo, they are about the size of a motor home pulling a U-Haul. Their horns start on their heads, swirl halfway down around their faces, and then curl back up at the ends. Sort of like a flip hairdo. (Think Doris Day in the fifties. Only Doris was cute.)

Water buffalo give new meaning to the phrase "whipped with an ugly stick," and their dispositions match. Here is my suggestion: if you travel to Africa and meet up with a water buffalo, don't make eye contact, for heaven's sake don't criticize their horns, and immediately make a beeline for the Canary Islands, (a herd of canaries are so much friendlier, feathers and all).

Without warning, our driver, who had momentarily slowed down, floored the Land Rover. Now don't miss this: think of a former agoraphobic who couldn't go to the store for peanut butter. And then he drove right through the middle of the buffalo herd. It was like something you see on television and you think, *No way. That didn't really happen. Must be trick photography.* Here I was, smack dab in the middle of this absurd adventure!

Had the driver said to me, "What do ya think, Patsy? Should I go for it?" I would have told him he would have to be out of his ever-loving mind to consider taking on a herd of wild animals. So I'm glad he didn't take a vote; the ride turned out to be a highlight of my trip. I mean, how many people can say they hydroplaned through a herd of stampeding water buffalo? It will look so good on my résumé.

Here's the best part. It happened so fast I didn't have time to work up a healthy case of panic. Besides, I was too busy bouncing my head against the inside roof while trying to watch the buffalo stampede on all sides of us.

The buffalo are probably still in therapy as I write this. "I dunno, doc. I was minding my own business, grazing on dinner when a white box full of wide-eyed creatures flew through the herd. Honestly, it took the curl right out of my horns."

Yahoo! A former scaredy-britches boot-scootin' over the savannahs of Africa . . . and loving it.

Yes, there is a God, and he obviously has a great sense of humor. Of course I have not always been able to have an adventure especially of that proportion and think it fun. My mind was so dimmed by Fear's dissertations that told me I was never safe that it took the hiding of God's Word in my heart before I began to see the way out of the shadowed life I had lived.

The opening quote to this chapter suggests that, if we are afraid, we should turn on the light. I couldn't agree more.

Turn on the light of God's Word. "For God has not given us a spirit of fear, but of power and of love and of a sound mind" (2 Timothy 1:7).

Turn on the light of faith. And risk taking the next step out of your self-imposed limitations. What do you have to lose? Fear? Go for it.

Turn on the light of your mind by believing what you can't see, which is that God holds you safely in his care no matter where you are and that he is unfolding his plan for your life. You can't travel outside his presence.

Turn on the light of friendship. Let others know when you are uneasy and then allow them to stand with you. It will comfort you, strengthen you, and keep you humble. We weren't meant to go this life alone.

And then turn on a light and book a flight, oh, let's say to India, and ride a painted elephant. Or to Switzerland and climb the Alps. It will look good on your résumé.

3

Ire Fire

Never go to bed mad. Stay up and fight.

Phyllis Diller

What coils your rubber bands into a flaming missile? Telemarketers? Taxes? Teenagers? Tardiness? Traffic?

We hear so much these days about road rage, which is a scary scenario. I remember a male stranger being infuriated because he thought my friend and I shouldn't have eased into his lane of traffic, even though he wasn't close and we had scads of room. The guy sped up and then went bonkers as he tried repeatedly to force us off the highway. He pulled in front of us and slammed on his brakes. Finally, at the last minute, we scampered off a ramp he had just passed. We pulled onto a side street and shook for a few moments before continuing on. If his goal was to intimidate us, may I say, "Congratulations, Madman, you succeeded!"

More times than I would like to admit, I've emotionally slammed on the brakes of my frustration in front of a loved one in an attempt to get him to hear me. I've tried to force that person off his road with a barrage of complaints and accusations so he would stop to pay attention, or I've done so as an act of retaliation.

I've learned it can take a lifetime to correct that kind of tire-screeching approach. It leaves skid marks on people's spirits, and they become self-protective and look for the nearest exit. And who could blame them?

Is it ever appropriate to be angry? Absolutely. It's just that anger needs boundaries, which don't include using four-wheel vehicles or ranting to make a point.

Scripture guides us toward more dignified resolutions, ones that leave others and us intact. I have found over the years that the boundaries from Proverbs of "kindness and truth" help us corral our anger and express our feelings in a way others are willing to hear. Not to mention that when these boundaries are set, they become stepping-stones in the building of our character.

Kindness is a way to express feelings that's more likely to be heard by others because it takes the *attack* out of truth. It also tests our motives, because being kind is very hard when we're bent on revenge. Kindness is more like an invitation into a garden, which is all about growth, not a shove into the back alley to pummel someone spit-silly.

Truth can be a bully. Have you ever been told the truth by someone who left you feeling beat up? I have, and I'm sure I've done that to others while thinking I was doing them a service.

Truth is imperative. It's our ticket to liberty. So I'm not saying to avoid it; I'm saying to approach it with compassion. No, not water it down so the value is lost, but allow the hearer the grace to process your words without being devastated by them.

We should always ask ourselves, "Is what I'm about to say wholly true?" "Wholly true" glimmers of Christ. And if it's true, ask Christ if you're the one who is supposed to say this truth to the other person. How would Christ have me offer this to the person in a peacemaking way? Timing and attitude are paramount.

When we put our words through the filters of kindness and truth, anger won't have a chance to exact a greater price from everyone involved. If our motive is to reconcile differences and not to offend our offender or to prove her wrong, then we will have a heart resolve that leaves us feeling settled and holds the potential for restoration of the relationship.

Last year I boarded a plane and was seated behind my friends Mary and Luci. Luci leaned over to the girl across the aisle and asked if she would mind changing seats with me. She was willing, and we quickly made the switch. In doing so, the gal ended up without a blanket. I already had taken mine out of its bag, so I kept it with me, thinking she wouldn't want a used cootie-cover. She flagged down the flight attendant, alias Attila the Hun, and asked for a blanket. Attila was ticked, which seemed to be her style of relating.

"Where is the blanket I put there?" the attendant demanded. "You had one. What did you do with it?"

I, feeling partially responsible for the girl's dilemma, stood up and chimed in, "Excuse me, but we changed seats, and I have that blanket. There was no blanket at her seat."

Ms. Hun spun around and spouted at me, "Get out of my way. I have work to do, and you're in my way."

I stepped in front of my seat and watched as she huffed away. I looked at the young woman, and she looked at me, both of us bewildered by the attendant's curt wielding of power that was so untypical of flight attendants. A little while later the attendant came by, threw a blanket at the girl, and stomped off.

As I thought about the inappropriateness of the flight attendant's actions, I felt I should address it. I waited, though, until I prayed. *Lord, if you place her back in front of my face, I'll take that as an opportunity to say something. And, Lord, you know I'll need your Spirit to do it in kindness so please guide me.*

Our plane was huge, with many flight attendants; so I knew I might not see her again. But lo and behold she came back some time later, leaned down, and asked, "What would you like for dinner?"

I told her my meal choice, and then I motioned her down to my face level. As I made eye contact, I said, "Do you think you were unkind earlier?"

"What?" she asked, taken aback.

I repeated the question, "Do you think you were unkind?"

"I was busy," she said emphatically.

"I'm aware of that. My question was, 'Do you think you were unkind?'"

"You were in my way."

"Were you unkind?" I calmly repeated.

Attila's cloak of superiority slipped off her shoulders as she leaned down close to me and whispered almost respectfully, "I'm sorry you felt I was unkind."

"Thank you," I said, trying to catch her downcast eyes.

I figured that was as close as the woman would ever come to ownership of her abrupt behavior. Then Attila straightened up, gathered her wits, pulled up her cloak, and said under her breath, as she quickly strode off, "But you were in my way."

After the "chat" between us, she became attentive and helpful, but only to me. Otherwise she remained surly and became the negative topic of the airplane chatter. How sad.

I suspect she wasn't voted the most popular girl in her school or employee of the month. And she probably seldom is invited to join others for lunch. I also wouldn't be surprised to hear that our flight attendant's heart had been crushed, that she had suffered great loss, and that she long ago ran out of tears from crying herself to sleep out of self-disgust.

I asked the attendant if she felt she had been unkind, rather than confronting her, because I thought it was a kinder approach. Also I was hoping, if she admitted her behavior, she might be nudged toward taking responsibility for her hostility. That way she could change. That's because, if we don't own it, we won't work at fixing it. Trust me on this.

Along with kindness and truth, Scripture also offers us a time boundary for our fury. It tells us not to let the sun go down on our anger. Now, that's a tough one, because when I'm angry, I don't take time out to set my watch.

I recently was in a less-than-attractive mood that I had been stirring the ashes over for days. That fire might have remained more contained if I had sat in my closet and smoldered. But no, instead I took my irritable self to the mall. After I shopped in one store for a while, I arrived at the checkout line to find no salesperson to help me. That annoyed me. Well, okay, okay, I had come in annoyed, and I had a growing desire to share it with someone.

The clerk who had been visiting with his friends finally noticed me and came over with a warm smile. I didn't return his offering. He tried to engage me several times in happy chatter until he noticed my inhospitable scowl. He stepped back and hurried to finish ringing up my items. After he bagged the books and handed me the sack, he thanked me. I half-acknowledged his politeness and was about to walk away when he said, "Did you know there's an author by your same name, Patsy Clairmont?"

My heart sank when I realized he might know me.

"Really?" I replied, trying to sound surprised as I backed away.

"Yes, have you ever read her books?"

At that point I was certain I heard a faint celestial giggle. Inside myself I replied, *That's not funny*.

Don't you hate getting caught?

May I just say that getting caught has a way of careening one into ownership, whether we want it to or not. Yes, I confessed to the nice man that I was the not-so-nice Patsy, and then I tried to imagine him explaining our encounter that evening to his wife, whom he had said loved my work. Words like *surly*, *cranky*, and *Attila* came to mind. He had every right to ask me, "Do you think you were unkind?"

Think about it: anger affects our appearance, our health, our sanity, and certainly our relationships. I mean, really think about it. Who was the last person you saw who was furious? How did he or she look? What was the outcome of the fury? Did that person win?

I believe that even if we "win," we lose. We exact a price for sustained angry behavior. It comes out of our health, our relationships, and our personal dignity.

When we recount our behavior later and tell how we let someone else "have it," which we often do in an attempt to justify our behavior or possibly to flaunt it, we sound shallow even to ourselves, like a nickel in a tin cup.

Did you ever play "hot potato" as a kid? Everyone passes a potato as quickly as possible around a circle, hoping not to be holding it when the timer goes off. Anger is a hot potato that we like to hand off.

Recently I approached a four-way-stop intersection in my hometown, came to a complete stop, and then, because no other cars stopped at the corner, I proceeded to cross the street. Suddenly a car approached one of the stop signs, and the driver laid on her horn but didn't attempt to stop. I slammed on my brakes, unsure what was going on but now aware of her car hurling toward me. The Indy wannabe swerved a few feet around the front of my car, while she indignantly shook her fist at me and mouthed some kind of salutation not found in the New Testament. She drove off feeling justified to have honked and ranted. In her estimation someone had entered her space, and, buddy, she wasn't having it. I thought to myself, as I eased on down the road, that she would drive through here again and then realize she had run a stop sign and had blamed me for her hot-potato reaction.

Later I recounted the experience to my husband, and on reflection I wondered how many times I had done that very thing in relationships, blaming someone else for my mistakes and then driving off feeling wronged. I'm learning to ask God first to lead and guide me into all truth before I go speeding off, shaking my fist at innocent bystanders.

So what is it that coils your rubber bands? What lights your fight fuse? We all have misused our anger either toward someone else or toward ourselves. I believe anger was given to us in an emotional wad so that we would have a way to vent injustices and offenses and not implode. Also, anger, when processed, can motivate us to make life-altering changes.

I giggled when I read Phyllis Diller's quote, "Never go to bed mad. Stay awake and fight." But the truth is, she's wrong . . . at least about her timing. It can be good to voice our issues so long as we're fighting fair. But once the sun goes down, we need to have said what needs to be said and then let go of those things we can't change. Or we should at least agree to disagree until further notice. To fall asleep night after night with the grumble of ire inside us stokes fury, and the next thing you know we become a version of, well, Attila the Hun.

4

Perils of Pauline

What I look forward to is continued immaturity followed by death.

— Dave Barry

Before movies had sound—yes, there was such a time when the only thing you heard at the show were Jujubes ricocheting off the screen in time to the music—there was Pauline. Actually, when I was a kid we had talkies (honest), but they would show silent clips at the theater as fillers between movies.

That was when I was introduced to Pauline, the innocent victim of treachery. The silent films I saw almost always included her. It made you wonder how one girl got herself into so many pitiful situations. She was a beautiful blonde with a tiny waist, big eyes, batty lashes, cute dresses, and she always needed to be rescued. She was a pity party waiting to be unwrapped.

A villain with a long, curled mustache, the tips of which he twirled between his finger and thumb, had tied the poor girl to the railroad tracks while a fast train approached. Or the petite darling would find herself in a runaway balloon, a burning house, or teetering on the edge of a cliff about to be pushed over by the devious scoundrel. Even though the only sound was background, choppy music, when Pauline screamed, you would swear you could hear her.

Pauline had the looks of fear and intimidation down to a finely honed craft, which attracted every hopeful hero for miles, usually Charlie Chaplin or the likes. Pauline gave the term "drama queen" dimension. Every girl left the show wanting to be a pitiful victim and every boy a he-man big shot. Hmm, talk about profiling.

"So what, Patsy?" you ask.

Well, as I remembered those overacted vignettes, I thought about how some of us easily fall into the damsel-in-distress role in real life—the backs of our hands over our mouths, our eyes glimmering with almost-tears, quivering voices, and weakened-knees attitudes. Yes, some of us are "stars" in our own right.

We Paulines tend to make life into suspense serials as we hop from crisis to crisis, some of our own making, crying out for heroes to rescue us. But what we actually need to be liberated from is our self-pity.

Pity is not pretty. Pity is emotional quicksand. I can think of no other feeling that will take you down as quickly.

Pity's mantra is "self"—how I feel, what I think, what I want. Though this is legitimate information, when taken to the extreme it becomes a nauseating yet intoxicating cocktail.

We convince ourselves that, if anything bad is going to happen, it will knock on our door first. We're sure no one has it as rough as we do. Then we set about trying to convince others of our futile plight.

We pity-ers feed on our tears, rehearsing our woes over and over again to anyone who will listen. Folks soon bolt for cover when they see us coming. And while we have all participated in self-pity at some juncture, quite honestly some of us are addicts, true veterans.

My husband has a most annoying habit when I whine. He stretches out his arm and then rubs his thumb and forefinger together as if he is playing the world's smallest violin for the world's largest whiner. How rude is that?

Actually, it's helpful (don't tell him), because I can whine and not even realize I'm doing it. That's how entrenched my habit is. Then I see Les across the room, his arm outstretched, and I think, *Uh-oh, I'm doing it again.*

Habits are hard to break, and whining is especially tenacious, a real Velcro buddy. Speaking of buddy, I have one friend who, if I begin to feel sorry for myself around her, will say, "Would you like a little cheese with your whine?" Cute. Not!

I learned to whine as a child. When whine is reinforced as an acceptable way to interact with others and to get what you want, you incorporate it into your behavior as a viable skill. You don't ask yourself if it's right or wrong; you just know it works. And because it worked as a kid, I took my well-honed craft with me into the adult world. Actually, by then it was second nature.

Whining is like nails on a chalkboard; nobody wants to hear it. It will never be joyous music to the ears of others, even if, like me, they're tone-deaf. Whining is sung in the key of "me" and has the ability to disband the choir. Eventually they tune us out and turn us off.

As a young adult, I felt sorry for myself because, as an agoraphobic, I couldn't do things other people could do. Even simple assignments like going to the grocery store, attending church, or riding in an elevator were too much for me. I didn't do bridges, tunnels, or amusement park rides. I didn't feel comfortable in crowds, on a boat, in an airplane, or in a car. And the list careened on. Don't you know I was a barrel of fun?

So you can see I had a lot of material to whine about. I was a tragic opera. Oops, there I go again. Did I mention exaggeration is another attribute of the whiner? We like to pump up our trouble with defeating words like "never," "can't," "won't," not realizing how it deflates our strength. I found if I whined long enough and loud enough I could whine my way into a pit of self, which I must say is not a spa-like environment.

Self-pity is a roadblock to maturity, not to mention that it keeps joy and potential friends at bay. Pity is tricky because, once we fall down the deep well of its anguish, we lose our ability to stop the momentum. That's why we must nab that nasty critter at the get-go. When we refuse not to indulge it, pity scampers away looking for attention from someone else. Here are some of the changes I had to make in order to shake loose this habit.

First I had to admit I was feeling sorry for myself (ownership). Second I had to ask forgiveness of the Lord and of others. And then third, I had to memorize verses that helped me when I felt myself begin to tumble ("For to me, to live is Christ . . ." Philippians 1:21), and I also had to deliberately make my way back up toward the light.

I would sing, recite, and often call a friend to pray for me when I felt myself slipping. It helped me to hear another person's prayers on my behalf. Besides, I wasn't sure if God had grown weary of my whiny voice, too, and maybe he would prefer to listen to my friends. (That's called weak theology.)

Living in self-pity is a shortcut to depression, and who wants to go there? No one volunteers for dungeon duty. Notice the word *dung* in dungeon. Eww.

I had to fight not to give in to the exhaustion that accompanied pity, so it didn't cover me in murky gloom. In my recovery I literally had to learn how to sing a new song and to step lively to a new life-dance.

I began to attend a Bible study, which was one of my step-lively moves, with other women in different stages of their personal growth. I found it helpful to observe how others coped with disappointment and handled relational pressures, because they seemed to have skills I didn't. Their results definitely were preferable to mine.

As I spent more time looking outside myself, I found ways to circumvent my whiny habit. One of the things I most admired about the Bible study women was that they purposed to praise, and that praise seemed to hold them in good stead.

I practiced praise, which started out feeling stiff and unnatural. In time it became a flow that brought healing to my mind and heart. Praise breaks up the repetition of whining, which is what that habit lives on.

So, if you're feeling pitiful, practice praise. And I encourage you to find some living examples of those who incorporate praise—you usually can recognize them by their glowing countenances and their sweet dispositions. Once you find them, sharpen your pencil and take notes.

Recently I met a true star of an example in an unexpected place. And trust me, I took copious notes. If I could right now, I'd take you to meet her, but you would have to pack a big suitcase because she lives on the other side of the world. And yes, expect multiple flights, the fifth one being a single-engine plane flown by a bush pilot over herds of wild animals. Then we'll switch over to a Land Rover, and I highly recommend you put on your seatbelt, because, honey, you are about to ride over some rugged terrain. This road has potholes, some of them the size of Rhode Island. A couple of more hours of rocky travel, and we arrive. Congratulations, you are at Rebecca's house. Er, hut. Oh, and by the way, we're in East Africa.

Members of the World Vision team, who assist children in third-world countries, introduced Rebecca to us. She has six children in her care. Three are hers and three belonged to her daughter, who is buried behind Rebecca's hut, a victim of AIDS. She is buried next to her sister, who died from AIDS the year before.

Rebecca's husband deserted his family, so the full responsibility rests on her shoulders. Her mud hut is empty, except for an unvented fire pit, sticks, a few thin throw rugs, a couple of blankets, and some hollowed gourds.

From all I saw and heard, Rebecca's life had been severe, and her losses were continuing as she had just received word that her youngest grandchild, who is three years old, has AIDS and tuberculosis.

Rebecca deserves a pity party. I would volunteer to throw it for her, but I didn't see even a trace of self-pity from Rebecca. Instead, she didn't so much as release a note of whine. In fact, she exuded joy. And if you've never seen the North Star's brilliance on a cloudless night, you would experience it on Rebecca's face every time she spoke the name "Jesus."

An interpreter asked Rebecca if she would show us her hut. She was thrilled, and she was proud that she had a roof over her family's head. World Vision recently had given the family several new blankets, and she had them hanging on stick-hooks on the wall. The blankets were obviously their most prized physical possessions. Oh, except for a well-worn picture postcard of the family who sponsored her son so he could go to school. She held it against her heart with affection. (Mothers are like that the world over—help our children, and we'll love you forever.)

We asked Rebecca what we could do for her, and she said, "I need nothing. I will pray for you." Don't miss what she said. Let me say it again, "I need nothing. I will pray for *you*."

That's what it means to leave a legacy for one's children and grandchildren. Demonstrate your faith in the midst of hardship, and they will remember your sterling example during their hardships. When times are hard, it's human nature to search our minds for what others have done to survive. Rebecca's children and grandchildren have a heritage because of her demonstrated faith.

I need Rebecca's prayers the next time I think my life is hard. The next time I feel inconvenienced and the next time I grumble about my cozy home, my well-stocked pantry, my king-size bed, my busy schedule, my doctor's full waiting room, my broken nail.

My, my, my. Deliver me, Lord, from my, mine, more, and me.

Yep, we all need a Rebecca in our lives to demonstrate for us the liberating beauty of gratitude that banishes whine and self-pity.

I wonder if Rebecca has been introduced to Old Testament Ruth. They share the attributes of courage and grace as they both walked a lonely road. Also, each had a giving spirit toward others while in the midst of her own pressing need. When we first meet Ruth, she doesn't have children; in fact, she is burying her husband and setting out on foot across a rugged terrain. Ruth's not alone. She is traveling with her mother-in-law, Naomi, whose heart is broken. So they walk in time to the tune of Naomi's dirge. Naomi is bitter, and she knows it. "Call me Mara, because the Almighty has made my life very bitter," Naomi announced when she arrived in her homeland (Ruth 1:20 NIV).

Ruth was committed to her mother-in-law's well-being and extended grace to Naomi, even when Naomi told Ruth not to come home with her. From the outset Ruth chose to follow Naomi's God, not Naomi's humanity.

Ruth's words of allegiance fall like stardust over their hardship, "Where you go I will go, and where you stay I will stay. Your people will be my people and your God my God" (Ruth 1:16 NIV).

Imagine young Ruth, after burying her loved one, leaving the safety of her homeland with a bitter relative with no idea what the future held for them. Ruth could have joined with Naomi to sing a sad duet. Who would have blamed her? But instead, the young widow sang a higher note; she sang of devotion, and then she broke into a heart-changing aria of trust in God: ". . . your God, my God."

Ruth couldn't have guessed God's unfolding plan as she stood weeping over her husband's fresh grave, as she traveled down a long road with Naomi, as she worked in foreign fields with danger lurking. Ruth had no way of knowing that she would marry again and conceive a child, nor that her child would become the great-grandfather of King David. Nor could this humble woman have known that she and her son would be in the direct lineage of Christ.

Dear sisters, we don't know what is in store for us either. But we do know that we want our song to be remembered for its winsomeness, not for its whine, for our faith, not for our faultiness. We don't want to live and die in immaturity.

Dave Barry says, "I look forward to continued immaturity followed by death." It's one of those statements that causes us to laugh and wince at the same time.

Who among us wants to die a pitiful Pauline and leave the legacy of a helpless victim? It takes hard work to leave victim behavior behind. But it's worth it. Effervescent Rebecca had every reason to fall face-first into her sorrows, but she has chosen instead to allow Jesus to be the Lifter of her Head and the Light of her path. Imagine the rich legacy this women who lives in utter poverty will leave her children and her grandchildren. I believe generations of her family will rise up and call her blessed.

I want my grandchildren to have a heritage that guides them to a higher path. Whining is the melody of immaturity. I want my grandsons to march strong and tall and praise loud and clear like Rebecca and the psalmist David.

"He . . . brought me up out of a horrible pit, out of the miry clay, and set my feet upon a rock, and established my steps. He has put a new song in my mouth—praise to our God" (Psalm 40:2–3).

Recently, while considering the honor of being a grandmother, I penned these words for my little ones that they might know their Papa and Nana's hearts for Christ and for them.

> To our darling grandchildren . . . who are tatted out of the very mercies of God's heart. You give us entrance into the future while we look toward heaven. You go and do wondrous things while we prepare to revel in another life.
>
> Follow the crumbs we have left for you . . . They will lead to a great banquet, a glorious feast, a holy supper, a divine Savior.
>
> May you realize early the gift of your trials and triumphs. Open your days with a grateful heart, keep their lessons near, for wisdom is borne out of pain, joy, failure, and success.
>
> Occasionally lean in and listen for the song we have left behind. We weren't always in tune, but we sang it in love, that you might have a reason to dance even in the midst of great losses.
>
> Papa and Nana

The pit of pity has no orchestra, but the whine drones deep, like the underlying tone of a bagpipe. And so we pray, "Lord, deliver us from the horrible pit of self-pity. Teach us words to a new song. Tune our hearts to your will. May the music of our lives delight you and cause your toe to tap and your hands to clap out of the sheer joy of seeing your children grow up. In your kindness remind us often that we are not helpless, that you are our helper and our rescuing hero, and that the choices we make in our lives and the songs we sing can be epistles to those coming along behind us. Amen."

5

Infinity Pool

Most of the important things accomplished in the world have been accomplished by people who have kept on trying when there seemed to be no hope at all.

— Dale Carnegie —

"We have given your sister every drug that might help. There's nothing more we can do. Her body is shutting down."

My only sister and only living sibling, Elizabeth, was dying, and no one knew why. It looked hopeless. Then, as I sat at her bedside telling her stories of when she was a child, as mysteriously as she had slipped into the coma, she began to wake up.

The doctors were mystified at my sister's recovery. They couldn't explain it; they just knew it shouldn't have happened. "She was too far gone," they told me. Then, after she was conscious, the doctors said she would be paralyzed, but she isn't. They thought she would be blind, but she isn't. The doctors studied her closely and walked away shaking their perplexed heads. The slopes of hopelessness are slippery, even for observers, and hard to climb back up once you have slid down the embankment.

Albert Einstein said, "There are two ways to live your life. One is as though *nothing* is a miracle. The other is as though *everything* is a miracle."

When I arrived at the hospital, Elizabeth's vital signs were dismal, but I didn't whisper my good-byes to her. It never seemed like the right time, as I sat at her bedside day after day. I didn't have a sense that she would be healed, but I didn't have a sense she would die. I pleaded for her recovery, and then I waited to see what God had planned.

When my sister's eyes flitted under her eyelids one morning, my heart flooded with fresh hope, and when she followed my instructions even before she was fully conscious, I wanted to tell the world. It was all I could do not to run up and down the hallways of the hospital shouting the news.

I wonder if that's how Martha and Mary felt when their brother shook off his grave clothes. Of course, Lazarus was dead, while my sister still had a feeble pulse.

My philosophy on hope is this: if there's any sign of life, there's hope for this life. If there's no sign of life, there's hope for the next life. Either way we win. Christ made sure of that.

I wonder if it's possible to fully describe hope or how it feels. I know hope feels bigger than my ability to hold it inside without becoming airborne. It activates fresh shipments of blood, energy, and gratefulness that seem to surge with holy force. Hope seems light like a wisp of down on a soft breeze; it's sparkling clean like a new sky after a spring rain. Hope is a baby's coo, a toddler's first step, a prodigal's return . . .

Wait . . . oh, now I'm getting it: hope is an infinity pool that has no boundaries and can't be contained. It can't be limited to a word, a phrase, a dissertation, or even a heavily-volumed library. Hope is eternal and, therefore, beyond us to define. Yet sometimes I see hope in a life, and when it's there you can spot it, even if you can't touch it or taste it, because hope is palpable.

We catch glimpses of hope in Helen Keller's story. Helen's life at the age of nineteen months took a radical turn when, after an illness, she was left blind and deaf. Later Helen would amaze the world with her story and achievements. She would say of her life, "I thank God for my many handicaps, for through them I have found myself, my work, and my God."

When Helen was six years old, her unguided behavior was out of control. Her well-meaning family had indulged this needy child, and she had become impossible. Relatives wanted Helen's family to put her away in an asylum. They saw no hope for a child who could not see or hear, who ate with her hands and threw fits.

Imagine what a tragedy that would have been if Helen had been taken away and forgotten about, not only for her, but also for her family, for us, and for the countless deaf and blind who benefited from her productive brilliance.

Unless we've been in emotionally pressing situations, we have no idea what it requires of individuals to hang in there when things look hopeless. Helen's mother, Kate, emotionally tattered yet tenacious, kept reaching out into the darkness, searching for a glimmer of hope. She made a trip to see a specialist in Baltimore, where the doctor cracked open the door of hope when he told them he believed Helen could learn. He then sent her to someone else.

Isn't that often how it goes? We go from one doctor to another, one job to another, one church to another, one Bible verse to another in search of a flicker of hope. One lit candle in a window gives us the incentive to carry on; that's all we ask.

Guess to whom the Baltimore doctor sent the Kellers? Alexander Graham Bell. It makes sense, though, doesn't it? Alexander was the fellow who transferred sound through a phone line, so he just might have ideas to help the deaf to hear. Brilliant.

Did you know that Alexander was also director of the Institution for the Deaf? I didn't. I also didn't realize he is credited with the invention of the respirator, metal detector, and some kind of gadget that detects icebergs, as well as many other inventions and accomplishments. In school, Alexander studied the science of acoustics. And the reason he followed that path was because he hoped to help his deaf mother to speak. Did I mention his wife was deaf too?

Anyway, Alexander had Kate Keller write to the director of the Perkins Institution in Massachusetts, and it was he who contacted Anne Sullivan, a former student, to see if she would be willing to work with Helen.

Consider how hard Kate worked to find a shred of hope for her precious daughter. We hear about Helen's amazing story, but behind the scenes is a mom scouring the earth to find help, to find hope. The Kellers weren't financially well off, and Kate worked on a plantation trying to make ends meet. So to take trips and search for doctors had to be a sacrifice, but the circuitous path she took brought them to a stunning miracle.

Anne Sullivan became not only Helen's tutor but also her lifelong companion. When Anne died, their secretary Polly Thomson stepped into Anne's place. Polly began working for Helen and Anne in 1914. Because of their constant companionship, they were known as "the three musketeers." In 1918, the trio flew to Hollywood to make a silent film about Helen's life called *Deliverance*. After the passing of Helen's beloved Anne, Polly was her natural replacement. Today the ashes of Helen, Anne, and Polly are deposited at the National Cathedral in Washington DC.

Hope can seem elusive. It must have appeared that way to Anne Sullivan, who lost most of her sight by the time she was five years old. Her mother died when Anne was ten years old. Her father, perhaps shattered or unwilling to assume sole responsibility for his family, disappeared, and Anne never saw him again. Anne and her brother were placed in a poorhouse where her brother died.

"Most of the important things accomplished in the world have been accomplished by people who have kept on trying when there seemed to be no hope at all." I wonder if Dale Carnegie wrote these words with Anne in mind. At least people like Anne, I'm sure; those who don't quit.

When Anne left the poorhouse, she pursued education at a school for the blind. While there, Anne underwent two surgeries, which restored some of her sight. Much later her eyes once again would fail her, possibly from all the reading Anne had done for Helen.

So you can see that Anne walked through crushing losses very early in her life before she saw hope for her future as Helen's teacher. Perhaps Anne's losses gave her the strength to hang in there despite the initially abusive behavior of Helen, who was acting out her indulged childhood, her boredom, and her frustration. Whatever shaped Anne, she was a woman of grit. The Kellers had found the right teacher for their daughter.

The day Anne finally had the big breakthrough with Helen is best told by Helen herself:

> We walked down the path to the well-house, attracted by the honeysuckle with which it was covered. Someone was drawing

water and my teacher placed my hand under the spout. As the cool stream gushed over one hand she spelled into the other the word 'water,' first slowly, then rapidly. I stood still, my whole attention fixed upon the motions of her fingers. Suddenly I felt a misty consciousness as of something forgotten, a thrill of returning thought, and somehow the mystery of language was revealed to me.

Following that moment of revelation, Helen tells how she ran from item to item wanting to know its name. Hope charged through her, electrifying her behavior. In the next couple of hours, Helen learned more than thirty new words.

Hope will do that for you. It opens you up so you can be full and brimming. Helen worked tirelessly the rest of her life, telling her story and offering lit candles for darkened windows.

Hope seems often to be birthed in tragedy, doesn't it? Last night on the news I heard a story about a nineteen-year-old man who had tried to end his life several years prior. Multiple losses had snuffed out his hope, and he couldn't see a reason to go on. So in a desperate moment, he took a shotgun, put it under his chin, and blew off the front of his face. But he lived. Doctors, at their own expense, agreed to remake his face. He has had countless surgeries, and through this process has found a purpose to live.

He now lectures at high schools, sharing his story of spiraling desperation and life-building recovery. With the suicide rate of our teens soaring, what a hope-bearing gift he offers. He still is deformed on the outside from the gun blast, but inside he's becoming whole. I applaud the courage of this developing champion of hope.

And speaking of a champion, when I met Jennifer Rothschild, a national speaker and an excellent writer, I was immediately drawn to her. She is charismatic, beautiful, intelligent, funny, kind . . . and oh, yes, she is blind.

Because Jennifer exudes hope and grace, it's hard to remember she has a disability and occasionally needs some assistance. I think she and Helen would have had a lot to talk about, and I bet the conversations would have been centered on what they could do, not on their limitations.

I think Jennifer's life-candle burns so brightly because she holds her disability loosely, not allowing it to define her—she leaves her definition to Christ.

Jennifer shares her faith not only in her spoken message but also by the hope-filled way she lives. She hasn't allowed her blindness to permeate her seeing heart.

We can't help but be drawn to hope. Thank you, Jennifer, Kate, Helen, Anne, Alexander, and Young Champion. We see your candles; they have helped add light to the world.

Hope is definitely an inside job. While we can't pump it up, we know it when it arrives. It fills the air with honeysuckle and fresh water. Hope shows us a better way, a higher path, a different perspective. It says yes even when doctors say no way. Hope gives "sight" to the blind. And "hearing" to the deaf. A future to the despairing. Hope reconfigures hearts. Redirects energies.

We not only pursue hope as a lifeline, but also hope pursues us. It is the essence of Christ. For, bottom line, Christ *is* our hope. "May the God of hope fill you with all joy and peace as you trust in him, so that you may overflow with hope by the power of the Holy Spirit" (Romans 15:13 NIV).

6

Chunky Monkey

Never eat more than you can lift.

Miss Piggy

Luci made me do it! Honest.

I'd never heard of a Caliche's until she said, "You and Les need to take a ride into Frisco's downtown and have a Caliche's (an ice cream concoction)." I do whatever Luci tells me . . . when it has to do with food anyway. She's an unofficial connoisseur and foodie.

Food, what an emotional magnet! It's a lifetime challenge . . . well, not for everyone. Some folks actually manage it just fine. Then there's me. If you even hint that I should consume yonder pie, I'm sprinting for a bib and utensils. What's that about?

Ecclesiastes says, "All man's efforts are for his mouth, yet his appetite is never satisfied" (6:7 NIV).

I can vouch for that. Seldom has one Krispy Kreme been quite enough, because two hours later I'm chin-deep in a vat of Ben and

Jerry's. Personally, I'm a Chunky Monkey fan. By the way, that's a confession, not a suggestion.

Therapists say eating is one of our earliest nurturing memories, and therefore many of us try to comfort ourselves with food. Hmm, I wonder if that explains the dumpster full of popcorn I inhaled last night? If food is comfort, I should be mighty cozy, but instead I feel weighed down with grocery guilt.

Groceries, though, are not my only habit. I wish. No, I'm an equal opportunity employer and also give too much time to game playing and mall hopping.

If I cut back in one area, I indulge in another. For instance, when I diet, I invariably become a reading machine. I can devour a good book like a bag of chips, which leaves me hungering for more. I find it hard to maintain my equilibrium, unless you count the bundle of books I have in one hand and an equally weighted bucket of store flyers for clothing items in the other "balanced."

I've found the reward system helpful. That's when I designate a certain slot of time for reading, or a game of Scrabble, or a visit to the mall, but first I have to accomplish real-life tasks. Sometimes I fast from a habit for weeks to help me moderate my tendencies. That's a good discipline for me.

For example, I tend to be a magazine addict, so I decided to give them up and use the money to help a child in a third-world country. That felt good. Besides, I can browse through magazines from time to time at a friend's house or the doctor's office.

Scripture says, "Make no provision for the flesh . . ." (Romans 13:14). That spoke to me of getting rid of some of the distractions that fritter away my precious time on this earth.

I wonder if that verse applies to our grocery list as well? I've noticed if I don't have it in my cupboard, I'm far less likely to have it on my hips. If I visit the mall less frequently, I won't be tempted to make an unnecessary purchase. And if I take a walk instead of a nap, I feel better . . . Well, you get the "make no provision" point.

Now, I realize that not making provision isn't always possible. For instance, if you have an active family, they usually require a full pantry. The troops might revolt if the shelf choices were limited to our latest diet attempts. Or guests probably wouldn't be impressed if we served up tofu roast doused in green tea.

"Eating rice cakes is like chewing on a foam coffee cup, only less filling," Dave Barry has noted. For some reason Les also shudders at our rice cake supply. I don't get his reluctance toward them. Who wouldn't want to eat foam orbs, especially since I toast them first? Well, okay, they don't really toast. It's more like an ebony scorch, but you hardly notice because I smear natural peanut butter over the blackened kernels. Oh, yum. Eat your heart out, Dave Barry!

The natural peanut butter is really an aerobic choice because after opening the jar, one must stir the floating oil slick into the peanut mortar. Warning: I have almost ruptured my massive biceps in the process.

Someone recently pointed out that biceps are supposed to be on the top of the upper arm, not reverberating off the bottom like laundry on granny's clothesline. Rude. Totally rude.

Ah, but I digress. Back to emotional eating. Most of us have grown up with celebratory eating. We feasted at Sunday banquets, holidays, birthdays, potlucks, when company came over, and even after funerals. When we're sick, what do people tell us? "You need to keep your strength up, go ahead take a bite, you can worry about your weight later, and don't forget 'to feed a fever' . . . hmm, or was that a cold?"

Well, you get the idea. Food (or shopping, reading, sleeping, etc.)

often represents more to us than just sustaining life. It reminds us of better times, family moments, wellness, and emotional connections.

Have you ever tasted a food that instantly flooded you with thoughts of someone? I did that the night I ate the Caliche's. With my first swallow, the banana pudding flavor registered "yesterday," and for a moment I was nine years old again, sitting in my mother's kitchen. Mom made the best banana pudding in the universe. Yup, universe.

It was lovely having that surprise Mom visit via food, until I got home and calculated the fat content of a Caliche's—about the same as the weight of a herd of Holstein, which was rapidly gathering moo-mentum around my midsection.

The rubber bands of guilt tightened, so I scurried out the door and hightailed it around the block at a breakneck pace in hopes of walking off my indulgence. A couple of times I even tried to run a few steps and was reminded why women my age no longer do that.

When I huffed and puffed my way back home, I settled down at my desk, grabbed a pen, and according to my best calculations, I might have worked off one tablespoon of that decadent delight. The other twelve tablespoons continue to, ahem, hang around.

Putting the brakes on an overdeveloped habit, whether that's eating, crafting, game playing, blogging, or television viewing, and then installing new ways to meet our emotional hunger takes repeated beginnings. It takes confession and forgiveness again and again. These activities aren't wrong until we choose to make them an obsession.

I have to guard against growing weary over my food failures, my computer habit, and my Scrabble sprees. Because if I give in to giving up, I throw caution to the wind, and that concerns me lest I outgrow my PT Cruiser, take shoe debt with me into the retirement center, or become permanently molded to my Mac mouse.

I think one of the keys to improving our existence is to selectively stock our pantries with foods that fill our souls. That way, instead of growing in width, we can grow in wisdom.

I don't know about you, but I learn best if I have a teacher. So I went in search of a pantry stocker and found one in the Old Testament: Abigail. This gal knew what it would take to sustain her strength even during an emotional famine.

Abigail's husband, Nabal, had moral and relational issues. For openers, he was surly, mean, selfish, and devious. But Nabal was rich in money, so when he said to those around him, "Let's eat," they filled their gold-digging plates. Nabal's power and intimidation were a force to be faced. The question was, who would have the fortitude to take on this bully?

Enter Abigail.

Fortitude feeds on the patience to sustain it. My impatience tendency would be to serve up for Nabal a sharp rap on his narcissistic crown with, say, a leg of lamb and suggest he shape up. But I don't recommend that approach. It's ineffective. Fun perhaps, but not honorable. Besides, why contaminate the lamb?

Abby, a wise woman, waited until the right moment to approach her heartless husband. I surmise Nabal was heartless because of his severe actions toward others, but he obviously had a heart because Scripture tells us "his heart died within him so that he became as a stone" (1 Samuel 25:37 NASB). He died a victim of his ingrown heart.

Think of the emotional reserves it must have taken for Abigail to endure the treachery of her scheming husband. Not only would she have needed patience but also discernment since his volatile temper could have spewed all over her—and probably had several times.

Abigail survived her difficult marriage with her brains, emotions, and dignity intact because, when it mattered most, she made excellent choices. That doesn't happen by wishing. She wasn't caught napping, channel surfing, or shopping for yet another headscarf to match her Liz Claiborne beaded sandals.

Something else that stood out to me was that Abigail didn't react out of her bruised emotions but out of her bright intellect. That's not to say she shut down emotionally, but she rose up to her tasks with her feelings following her life of faith. She already had a reputation for using her head, as my dad would say, "for something other than a hat rack."

In the midst of her crisis, instead of hiding in her pantry, burying herself in a good book, losing herself in her scrapbooking, or quivering with fear, Scripture tells us Abigail pulled out of her pantry bread, wine, sheep, grain, raisins, and figs. It said, "She lost no time" but immediately had food loaded onto donkeys and taken to David and his men as an offering (1 Samuel 25:18 NIV). She retained her personal dignity even in the shadow of her husband's public failures. Honey, that's not easy.

Note that Abigail was prepared for a crisis, otherwise she would have had to send her servants scurrying on those donkeys to Sonic to fill saddlebags with takeout. Instead, Abigail already had all she needed for an emergency. Note that she didn't wring her hands, argue with God about the injustice of it, or snap her rubber bands at the people around her. Instead, she lost no time. That tells us she was mentally alert, not an emotional muddle-brain.

I get muddled when I waste time instead of stocking my larder. I've been known to put things off until the arrival time draws near for dinner visitors, then I'm frantically running around in knotted circles. When my guests arrive on my front porch, I'm frazzled and embarrassed as the dreaded doorbell rings out my name, "Ding-a-ling."

Trust me, it pays to have a full pantry, and I'm not talking Caliche's. Abigail had stored up the bread from above, the wine of God's Spirit, the humble heart of a lamb, and the fruit of righteousness. If we did an inventory of Abigail's pantry, I wonder if it would look something like this:

Dignity—I have found dignity comes as we embrace our heritage in Christ and as we choose to do what is ours to do. (Go clean out that messy closet, clear that debris-strewn desk, apologize for your last hasty words, and feel dignity rise up within you.)

Discernment—While this is a gift, it also is worked into our hearts as we learn from our mistakes and seek God's counsel. Also as we observe people rather than judge them (Proverbs 18:15).

Intelligence—This is showcased as we apply God's Word to our own hearts before we offer it to others and when we think before we speak or react.

Self-control—Place balanced boundaries on your choices. And purpose to press the balance button on your habits again and again.

Preparedness—We've dusted our ducks and lined them up. We've made healthy provisions with the fruit of the Spirit.

Fortitude—This involves internal resolve for whatever arises regardless of the difficulty level. We recognize we have eternal reserves from which to draw.

Patience—We express a holy hush, demonstrated by our willingness to wait on God's timing. We give up our right to have things scheduled to our liking.

Humility—I believe this is the inner strength to serve with grace. I can't help but think of Sister Wendy Beckett when we mention humility. She is the nun known for her unique twist on fine art. She's often featured on the Public Broadcasting System (PBS). Sister Wendy lives under the protection of the Carmelite nuns in a trailer on their grounds in England. Even though she doesn't belong to the order, she follows their lifestyle when she is in residence. The sister is allowed to work two hours per day while the remainder of the day is devoted to prayer, silence, and solitude. Sister Wendy speaks only to the monastery prioress and the nun who delivers her provisions each morning. She says of solitude that it is something "chosen and loved."

Vain people don't choose solitude. They depend too highly on our mirrored responses to feed their egos. Usually those who have made peace with God and themselves seek the life of contemplation. Silence is a powerful and strict teacher that quickly reveals the heart's motives.

The above qualities were probably worked into Abigail's character as she endured the humbling experience of a tumultuous marriage, as she purposed to make wise choices despite Nabal's poor ones, as she didn't flaunt her wealth, as she sensed when to speak and when to remain silent, as she learned when to bow down and when to rise up.

I like spending time in Abigail's pantry because it makes me hunger to be that kind of a woman—one who isn't driven by her physical appetites. I've noticed when I tuck stories like Abigail's onto the shelf of my inner pantry, they help to safeguard me against the next time my life is topsy-turvy and I'm tempted to eat my weight in caramel sundaes . . . at the mall.

7

Shoe Goo

It always rains on tents. Rainstorms will travel thousands of miles, against prevailing winds, for the opportunity to rain on a tent.

— Dave Barry

No, shoe goo isn't something a cobbler uses for repairs on your high-heeled platforms; nor is it that last wad of bubble gum you had to pry off your loafers with a sharp stick. Shoe goo is that goopy gunk called *moodiness* that attaches itself to our personage.

I've observed that some of us are more given to sporting shoe goo than others. Have you noticed individuals with certain temperaments just have an innate spring in their steps, a jiggle to their wiggle, a throttle on their waddle, no matter what befalls them? I like to think of them as being in denial, which should alert you that I'm a shoe goo girl. I'm light-years ahead of where I once was when I sloughed through my daily life with the enthusiasm of an empty cardboard box. But still, moodiness likes to stick around me.

While certain personality types naturally are optimistic, others are given to bouts of melancholy. Sometimes it's an innate character design; other times it can be the result of a sad childhood, a disappointing adult life, depression, an accumulation of loss, or a self-serving habit.

I'm not a doctor, a psychologist, or a prophet, but I've been a moodologist (which means I have the skills set to be difficult to live with). So I would like to share with you some of the ways I've found to help me not to take the escalator down into the dumps every time things don't go my way.

Oh, don't get me wrong, these suggestions aren't magic. They won't cause us moodists to start skip-to-my-looing around the house. At least not immediately. But they might help us to find ways to improve our existence. And I'm not saying it's easy to change, especially at first. Few things can scrape the goo off our souls.

1. *Recognize we have choices.* This is important to remember when it comes to the blues . . . or browns or rusts. We can choose not to gloom a room. We can't always choose how we feel, but we can choose how we behave despite the fits our emotions might be throwing. Mood swings aren't stronger than our wills. Our wills may be underdeveloped from lack of purposeful effort, but we can change that. The will is a muscle that grows stronger with use.

(By the way, if you have been diagnosed with depression, these suggestions might not help you. Please don't be defeated with your progress, but stay current with your doctor and counselor. I'm not in any way trying to simplify what may be a complex journey for you.)

2. *Know yourself.* To the best of your ability, weigh your motives.

Warning: Girls, be alert because moods have feet. Yup, you read it right. Actually, they use our feet. We offer them transportation every time we give in to the weight of sadness, manipulate via our gloom, or sit under the spell of melancholy. We then walk our shadowy behavior through our day, which is one of the reasons we can "de-feet" them. Since we are the ones who transport them, we can choose to step out of our moody sandals and leave the shoe goo behind.

How many times have you said to someone, "Are you okay? You seem sad. Is something wrong? Is there anything I can do?"

Moodiness is readable about a block and a half away, which means it's a large-print emotion that can serve a purpose: it grabs people's attention, or at least the attention of those who care how we're doing. I don't deny that enough sad is in this world to make us authentically miserable; yet when some of us get sad goo on us, we can't seem to shake it loose as other folks do. We don't know how to get on with things. Before long everything seems to set off our negative meter.

Are we trying to capture the other's attention or to control that person with our moodiness? If we answer the latter, it's an unhealthy way to maintain relationships, as it tends to keep us stuck. Not to mention that we become an undesirable companion . . . And that, my friend, makes us feel really moody. Sad can glom on to us with little help, but when we indulge that emotion, the goo flows like lava.

Ask yourself, "To whom am I drawn? With whom do I want to spend time?" I bet they aren't gloomy. Enough said.

Did you notice that we're less cute when sad settles on our faces? Even wrinkles look fun when we smile; we look crinkly, not cranky. A smile is neon in its appeal, not to mention a powerful influencer. Haven't you been in a not-so-good mood and didn't feel like grinning, but then a stranger bebops past you and beams her bright-whites, and you find yourself returning the smile? What a great contagion to spread! May it catch on worldwide.

Recently I opened a container of cottage cheese, and on the inside peel of plastic were these words: "A smile is a gift anyone can give." I read it, and guess what? I smiled. I thought, *A smile is a wordless way to spread joy.*

My four-year-old grandson, Noah, is the baby of the family and tries to take full advantage of that position, which includes pouting. He has learned to drop his bottom lip halfway down to his Nikes. If that strategy produces the results Noah intended, he is quick to use it again. A purposed pout needs admirers, or it just isn't worth the lip-sagging effort.

I recommend asking the Holy Spirit to help you spotlight your pouty intentions. I can be so covert in my sadness that it seems appropriate to me and even deserved. I need the holy scrutiny of God's Spirit to help me to examine the truth within myself.

3. *Enlist a prayer partner* who will hold you accountable to change. Make it someone who has more follow-through than mercy and more kindness than criticism. I confess I sought a prayer person who was dripping in mercy, which both helped and delayed my progress.

4. *Watch what you watch.* Huh? Yup. I'm subject-sensitive when it comes to television and movies, and I bet some of you are wired that way as well. For instance, I don't do well with biographies of serial killers or investigations into crime scenes. I'm probably one of the few people in the world who isn't into *CSI.* Often I find the topics troublesome. Everyone is different, which is why you need to figure out what drags you down. I don't do violence, and I don't do scary shows, because I feel that the world has enough frightening elements, thank you. I even have to be careful of shows that do good things for hurting people, if they play up the tragedy too much, which is their temptation since tears sell. I tend to absorb the family's pain, and then I walk away, taking a heavy spirit with me.

Hmm, that doesn't leave me much to view. I now choose, instead of a shoot-'em-up show in the evening, the Home and Garden channel, a crossword puzzle, a good book, or gentle music.

I tend to have spells when nothing bothers me and other times when many things are emotionally disruptive. Be sensitive to yourself. Not indulgent, but aware. If your emotions swing easily, help yourself stabilize by making balanced choices. We don't want to become so legalistic in our disciplines that we make ourselves neurotic and total bores.

5. *Choose to talk when you've sealed yourself off in silence.* Don't use silence as a weapon against others. It can be a control club that leaves invisible yet real damage in relationships. Angry silence harbors brooding, and brooding erodes character.

I had a relative who would come to visit our family, and whenever she was unhappy, which was often, she would slip a silencer on her guilt gun as she rocked her hurt feelings. The sound of that creaky rocker could be heard for miles. It was the loudest, most punishing quiet you've ever heard.

If you have developed the habit of using silence as the way to announce your displeasure, it will take effort and time to break through those self-constructed barriers. Speaking kindly when we feel stuck in sad shoe goo will be a liberating step.

For some reason we who advertise our pain with silence think others need to know we're miserable. We would be shocked to learn how many people have multiple hardships, but these folks still smile daily at others. They have purposed to compartmentalize their pain. By that I mean they take what hurts them, after they have done all they can do about it, and mentally set it on a shelf until an appropriate time to circle back and pick it up again. They don't take it to work, church, or the store to punish others with it, nor do they wear their pain like a cumbersome cloak.

For years I allowed my sadness—with the help of her neighbors, shame and guilt—to select my wardrobe. I refused to buy nice clothes for myself, because I felt I didn't deserve them. My clothes were frumpy and fit how I felt.

Today, when I see gals who have *worked* to look poorly, my heart aches for them. I know they are in a bad place, a sad place that's convinced them not to even try. We don't have to shop high-end to look cared for; we just need to take the time to make sure we are clean, smell good, have pressed our garments, mended any tears, and treated stains. While that sounds elementary, it isn't when you've worn sad so long you've forgotten you matter.

Years ago a mentor gave me advice that still rings true: "Do the best you can with what you've got, then forget yourself and get on with life."

6. *Avoid being verbose about your condition.* Earlier I said don't use silence as a pistol, but another weapon is a barrelful of words. I have done this. I also have misused silence. I'm a multi-mouth given to eruptions, which isn't unusual for those of us in a rubber-band wad.

When we go on and on about ourselves, people lose interest in a hurry. Verbosity isn't a gift. Many gifts are enhanced, if not dependent, on good communication skills. Yet, when we fill the air with an onslaught of complaints, not only does it drains the energy out of those who can't escape listening, but it also dulls their receptivity to us. We lose the legitimacy of our pain by our incessant need to broadcast it.

Sometimes, when I begin to chatter, I am attempting to untangle pent-up nerves. God bless the person who is willing to allow me to unwind.

My friend Janet called recently, and when I heard her voice, I unloaded my week on her. I became aware of my blathering, but I was speed-talking so fast I had trouble finding my brakes. I finally skidded to a stop and realized my flurry had to have been tiring for Janet because, for heaven's sake, even I was exhausted. After a silent moment I asked, "So, Janet, how was your week?" Concisely and quietly she told me, and it was worse than my news.

Afterward I thought, *Janet's approach was the healthy way to respond.* She waited to find out if I wanted to hear by my inquiry; then she answered in fifty words or less, and if I asked more, she then would share additional details.

We miss out on a lot when we're doing the majority of talking. Besides, I find that when I use my words to release emotions, it actually can frazzle me more. Or if I keep rehearsing all the minutia of an offense, like some who keep retelling how they acquired an old war wound, I only depress myself and keep my moodiness nourished.

People who have heard me speak are surprised to learn that my friends consider me quiet. I've practiced shushing myself so long that I rather enjoy hearing others blather—I mean share. Oh sure, I still have moments when, like a fire hydrant, I'm gushing words, but generally I've learned the art of listening rather than speaking.

Okay, let's review how to *de-feet* our moodiness:

1. Our wills are powerful. We can choose how we behave. We don't have to be a victim to our emotions, nor should others have to be.

2. We don't have to wear our sadness like this year's fashion statement. We can deliberately don kindness and compassion for others. This will help us to step out of ourselves.

3. Enlist a prayer partner.

4. Watch what you watch. Monitor the types of stimuli around you. Don't work yourself into a mood by what you view or listen to.

5. Break your silence. Bash down your self-constructed barriers. Every time we win over a bad habit, we're one step closer to liberty.

6. Relax—not everything we think needs to be formed into words. Remember, the Tower of Babel didn't stand. Conserve your energy, preserve your friendships . . . shh.

I've found memorizing verses on joy helps to protect my mind when I slip toward gloomy. I'm also affected by music; so I encourage you, if you love music, to sing songs that lift and calm your spirit. King Saul, when he was in terrible moods, would send for David to play his harp to soothe the king's spirit.

One last suggestion: if you have someone in your life who drags you down, take a vacation from the relationship until you have the skills and enough self-definition to relate to him or her differently. If it's someone you can't escape, read *Boundaries* by Henry Cloud and John Townsend. The principles are invaluable for all our relationships.

Remember, never stop trying to break habits that have you stuck in the muck, and don't give up on finding solutions to your internal conflicts. Shake that goo off your shoe and walk on!

8

Mourning Dew

Grief makes one hour ten.

—William Shakespeare

My heart is tugged by the significance of a cross that marks the spot. The cross is small and wooden, and a stuffed toy of a football player dangles from it. That marker resides outside my subdivision, so I see the miniature sign of death every time I leave home. Someone died in that place. Someone who was loved, and by the looks of the memorabilia, was a teenage boy. Those who cared for him, who can no longer hold him, reached out to touch the place of his departure. They needed a starting place for their grief.

I wonder about that football player's family. I wonder if they ever drive by that sad spot. I wonder if the ache has lessened for them. I wonder if their hearts are as splintered as the wood on that little cross? Actually, I'm sure they are.

I know the ache remains. That's not a secret. You see it in the eyes of every family who must say good-bye too soon. And no matter the age, it's too soon.

Death makes us wonder. We wonder what life is really all about. We wonder if God cares that our hearts are broken. We wonder why he takes someone we love. Not only do we wonder, but also we wander about in the valley of shadows for a time, trying to work out within us all that it means. Often we come out of the shadows with two things: a dull ache and a deepened resolve to live and love more attentively in the days we have left.

When my mother died three years ago, I found myself on the top wrung of the family ladder. That was sobering. And I was startled to realize I was an orphan. Even at my age that made me feel sad and tipsy. Tipsy and ladders aren't a safe combination.

I've said good-bye to many loved ones, as probably you have, and I've noticed that the older I become the more I think about those who have gone on. But death isn't the only loss we live with, although it may feel the most severe.

My friend Carol has buried a son; she watches today as a grandson struggles with a debilitating disease; and she has had many health struggles, including breast cancer. She is well acquainted with grief.

I recently asked Carol how she felt when she lost her hair during radiation and chemo. She recounted those days through tears because it stirred up tender moments of sadness and fear. She said that hair loss is traumatic more in thought than in reality. The dread of her hair falling out caused Carol nightmares, and she was jolted when she held fists full of fallen hair. But instead of dreading each descending strand, she contacted a beautician acquaintance. The gal came to Carol's house, and in the privacy of Carol's own room, the beautician shaved Carol's head. She said it was a liberating act. She felt as though she had regained some sense of control by having the hair loss happen in her time frame.

Losing one's hair is alarming, especially for us gals. Carol said it's not just about beauty, but she also had to wear hats to bed through the winter to keep her head warm. She wore wigs, but they made her head hot and itchy. And she said you are always aware that others know your tresses are faux.

Carol said there came a point when she dried her tears and settled into her loss because she knew her lost locks would have an eventual good ending: her hair would grow back. But what was more lingering was the nagging understanding that the cancer could return. The loss of her health security was the most troubling.

Don't tell Old Testament Samson that I think hair loss is harder on girls than guys. His haircut left him helpless, blind, and imprisoned, and eventually it cost him his life. And to think it was the love of his life who sharpened the scissors that felled the mighty man. How crushing.

No doubt about it, life is full of sorrow. From hair follicles to heart fractures, loss can be staggering. Henry Ward Beecher said, "Tears are often the telescope by which men see far into heaven."

I have a new neighbor, and one day we met on the curb for a first time chat. She told me her husband had died a year prior, and she was downsizing. I could see sadness brimming in her eyes, but I also saw courage mounting. She was taking important steps alone, and while it wasn't easy, especially the decision making, it was necessary for her well-being.

I was at a clothing store recently, and the lady in the next cubicle and I started a conversation. She told me she had been in a car accident that ended the life of her husband and left her body broken with extensive injuries. She had to temporarily set the grief of her husband's death on a shelf, while she used what strength she had to fight to live and endure her physical pain.

This gal had been going through waves of sadness and change that had left her questioning and sometimes angry. Unexpressed grief doesn't leave us; instead it waits to rise up another day to take our breath away. If we don't step through it, the grief will put on anger's clothes and create havoc.

One friend told me that after the death of a loved one she would go through her empty house and scream to release pulsating emotions. "It was that or implode," she confessed. "I felt as though I would lose my mind, because the agony was so intense. Screaming gave me an outlet to take the edge off the immensity of my emotions."

Venting is necessary. How do you vent?

William Shakespeare suggests, "Give sorrow words. The grief that does not speak whispers the o'er fraught heart, and bids it break."

Venting helps us to lower our pain level so we can make room for healing. Talking can help, support groups are valuable, exercise gives some physical relief, gardening or other types of life-giving activities provide distractions to give a bit of a break to our overprocessing minds, journaling can be cathartic, time really does help in the mending, and crying releases emotions and toxins. "Tearless grief bleeds inwardly," says Christian Nevell Bovee.

Who is more known for loss than Job? This Old Testament man lost everything and everyone except his wife.

I think Mrs. Job gets a bad wrap as an insensitive helpmate. We have to remember she had lost all her children too. While psychologists have whittled our grief responses into a tidy list of stages, grief is anything but tidy. I think the list is helpful, but it doesn't solve our pain or explain the different timetables each of us experiences.

Mrs. Job may have been hysterical and panicked when she cried out to her husband, "Curse God and die!" Who knows what we might say in the midst of a catastrophic loss? Are we really surprised that surging anger gushed forth?

Her comments contain her humanity. We never need God more, yet there may never be a time we understand him less than in our grief.

Our losses draw our raw emotions to the surface. We find our tears and even our laughter. It may sound startling to speak of laughter in a chapterful of pain, but it's a great relief to both laugh and cry. Those two responses live close to each other. Sometimes we have to laugh so we can cry, and other times we can lose our ability to laugh until after we've bawled our hearts out.

Carol, while going through treatment for her breast cancer, told me that her young granddaughter was curious about her wig. So Carol picked up just a corner of it on top so her granddaughter could get a peek. But on seeing her grandma's movable hair and her hairless head, the child was aghast and showed her displeasure. Carol, realizing that her slick new finish was more than this little girl had space for, reached out to comfort her and hoped she would soon forget. But Carol was so tickled by her granddaughter's innocent reaction that she had to run for the restroom where it was safe to guffaw loudly.

Make space for laughter in your grief; it takes more than just the edge off your pain.

God pieces together our broken stories of tragedy into beautiful substantive content. In Philippians Paul speaks of "the fellowship" of pain (3:10). Suffering is like learning a new language—we now understand how others feel, we know how to speak to their needs, and we know when to offer the sterling gift of silence.

My heart is tugged by the significance of it. The cross marks the spot. It's a wooden cross that's so small for what it once held—the weight of the world's sin. It's no longer a sign of death but of life because of our resurrected Savior. Tears are shed at the cross, tears of gratitude—gratitude that we are forgiven and that we are forever companioned. And one day every tear will be wiped away. Thank you, Jesus.

9

Breathing Space

Who will tell whether one happy moment of love, or the joy of breathing or walking on a bright morning and smelling the fresh air, is not worth all the suffering and effort which life implies?

{ Erich Fromm }

Emotions need space, or they forget the simple rules of breathe-in, breathe-out. We can get so excited, overwhelmed, or preoccupied that we simply forget to exchange the stale air in our lungs. When we're experiencing grief or other types of stress, we unconsciously breathe shallowly. Just as it's helpful to have a prayer place, we need spaces to inhale and exhale. They may be the same place, and they may not.

I adore my fun-loving husband. We've been married since 1962 before push-button telephones and electronic calculators hit the market. So we've been "hanging out" together for a mighty long spell. One thing we've both learned is that sometimes we need breathing space from each other. Yes, I just said that aloud. If Les had the chance, he would add "amen" to that statement while directing Handel's "Hallelujah" chorus.

Every now and again I will sweetly ask my retired husband, "Honey, don't you have somewhere you need to go?" Or he will say to me, when I've been off the speaking circuit for a while, "Dear, shouldn't you go somewhere and speak to someone other than me?"

An individual once asked me, "Doesn't that hurt your feelings?" Heavens no. I understand the need to have space to get sane. Sometimes we need emotional breathing room.

Les loves the television on, but I love music on. Les likes to make good use of a rocking chair, while all that swaying makes me dizzy. We tend to be on different eating cycles during the day and on different food programs, so coordination is a constant effort. We both enjoy the front page of the newspaper first, and we both like to do the crossword. Therefore, on occasion, a breathing space between us feels good. Not long, you understand, just a smidge of time to inhale and exhale. I don't want Les to go any farther than, say, Starbucks or Home Depot. Trust me, I have his cell number, and he has mine.

We all need breathing space from our routines, relatives, and other relationships. But here's my biggest struggle: how to get away from *me*. I often get on my own nerves. When I start to gripe at myself, I sometimes head for the beauty parlor, maybe because it's such a girly thing to do. Of course I enjoy the personal attention and usually the results. Besides, it gives me a mini breathing space.

I also love a long hour in a bookstore—okay, make it two. I love to roam the aisles to see what's new, what's old, and what's relevant for me. I like the freedom of leafing through volumes of books on multiple topics. I love to skitter through a stack of magazines to see if there truly is something new I haven't already seen a hundred times before. Make that a thousand. I mean, really girls, how many ways can we organize our closets? Yet I confess I enjoy the investigation of a new theory. Then there's the music area where one can don headphones and listen to anyone from Bocelli, to Bono, to Bing Crosby. And the sweetest bookstore experience is watching a child select a new read. Now that's precious, as they ponder the covers, riffle through the pictures, and then beg their mommies for their newfound treasures. Yes, I can really get lost in a bookstore.

I think every woman should have a lost-in-space place. It needs to be something you do and somewhere you go that not only pleases your senses but also results in satisfaction. What a reprieve for our emotions to have something to look forward to in the midst of the hustle and bustle, even if it's just to take a few moments to flip through the pages of a home magazine or to sink into the wonder of a well-woven tale. After a few pages of walking around in someone else's fiction, our reality seems easier to face. I'm not sure why that is unless it serves as a distraction that allows us to unplug from our own pressures for even a chapter or two. After a good read I seem to breathe easier. Last week to unplug I went for my first professional facial, which had to have been invented by angels on a sabbatical. It was heavenly.

Yet sometimes what I need most as a woman is to plug into others. One way I do this is via e-mail. Actually, girlfriends are a lifeline. Yes, they can contribute to some of my emotional knots, but more often than not they resuscitate me.

As the great philosopher Winnie the Pooh pontificated, "It is more fun to talk with someone who doesn't use long, difficult words but rather short, easy words like, 'What about lunch?'"

I challenged myself to make a list of how I've received fresh oxygen from others. I encourage you to make a list of your own. Here's mine:

Friends help us think. When I move the furniture around in my living room, one of the ways that helps me decide if I like the new layout is to go upstairs and look over the balcony into the living room. Placements I missed when I was *in* the room I now can see more clearly from this perspective.

Friends are like that. They often bring a different perspective that opens up a new view. Sometimes I'm so caught up in a moment that I don't see the bigger picture, but balcony friends call out to me what they see.

Friends help us hear our inconsistencies and pinpoint blind spots. I'm not suggesting that's fun, but it's valuable. We are all myopic when it comes to ourselves. And we all need accountability; otherwise we can be tossed into the vortex of our own opinions and drown in our littleness. Friends help to pull us out of small spaces. Even when they share their struggles, it can give our fears wings as we realize we aren't the only ones, that we're not alone in our emotional complexities.

I was griping about a relative recently to a friend, and she verbally nudged me into a place of seeing that what I was complaining about was a quality within myself that I hadn't owned. Now, that really wasn't fun! But, alas, it was bull's-eye accurate.

Friends rally when the winds of hardship bluster across our paths. My friend Carol told me that during her chemo treatments, she was sick and weak. Her hubby, Bruce, was trying his best to keep up with the housework, food preparation, and doctor/chemo visits. Her friend Ruth saw the need, and she and her daughter filled it by preparing and dropping off meals. Carol said it was manna from heaven and a tasty change of pace from pizzas.

When our family went through a trauma, we took turns helping each other to stay steady. And when my emotional knees would buckle, my friends would sprint to my side and hold me up with their presence, prayer, and wise whispers.

Friends believe in us. They applaud our gifts, and they celebrate our good fortune. When we have crushed spirits, we have a hard time believing we have anything to offer others. Then friends come into our life circles and announce that we have value and that our gifts are treasures. Initially we want to believe them, but it feels risky. I've been fortunate to have a parade of friends who were secure enough in their own gifts that they could point out and celebrate mine.

Friends aren't perfect and may not be forever. It's important that we not abuse our friendships by expecting them to do for us what Jesus plans to do another way. Remember that his ways and ours are further apart than Earth is from Saturn (930 million miles).

We will need tons of grace to endure the inadequacies of people in general and friends specifically. They weren't meant to be the end-all in "being there." That would be Jesus, who promised us, "I will never leave you nor forsake you" (Hebrews 13:5).

People not only will disappoint us, but many also will leave us and we them. We humans never are prepared for feeling rejected, abandoned, or replaced, but quite honestly, it's part of the human dilemma. We don't expect a friend to clock out, but it happens . . . and perhaps for the best. That's hard to grasp in the midst of misunderstanding and hurt.

Is our pain worth the risk to have friends? I wouldn't say I've entered the winter of my life, but I'm wearing a muffler and mittens. In all these years I've had many friends. Some are still in my life, and others are not. Some left because they needed to, and I understand that better today than I did earlier. My friends add so much joy to my world; so I would encourage you to take the risk to be friendly, even though the friendship may be only for a season.

My caution would be not to expect more of a friend than she can give. My expectations have been too high at times, and that only leads to disappointment, ill will, and exhaustion.

Oh, and one more thing about friends: they allow *us* to invest in *them*. Friendship should include reciprocity. If your friend is doing all the giving, she will wear out, and you will miss the satisfying pleasure of blessing her. I've had some chances to invest in others over the years. Take a look at this letter I wrote to Carol during her cancer treatments. It felt really great to be there for my dear friend in her time of need and hearten her with kind words.

To my artistic buddy,

I know this has been a very difficult journey—your body has been assaulted by both disease and technology, and yet you have been so brave. I know you haven't always felt brave, but you did what was given you to do . . . and you did it well.

Now you're at a new door, which takes courage to step through as well, but I believe that "He who has begun a good work . . . will complete it" (Philippians 1:6).

Being afraid is often the emotion we feel just before we dig deeper into our arsenal of faith. Fear often is the motivator that causes us to trust God in ways we never did before. And fear's power to rob us diminishes in the presence of faith.

To know you are one among millions in your health battle is both encouraging and discouraging. Yet you aren't another number to the Lord. He's been keeping an eye on you since he formed you, and he's not about to look the other way now.

So much of life is about relinquishment—giving up our

plans for his. Not easy, not fun, and often not what we had in mind. Perhaps, instead of asking, "Why me?" we should ask, "What would you have me do? Who would you have me talk to about you?" (A doctor? A nurse? A patient?)

If I had a magic wand . . . well, you know what I would do. I'd pull off a miracle for you. Here's the good news: God still performs miracles and doesn't require a wand. Often the ones he initiates are in the heart, but I know you know that.

I just want to say that, even though I'm down here in Texas for the winter, I continue to cheerlead in your corner. I read a quote by one Charles Beard, who said, "When it's dark enough, you can see the stars." Look up, my friend. I love you, and I want you to be restored.

Isaiah 45:3 says there are "treasures in darkness." Don't dash through this dark season and leave the treasures behind—bring them with you for the rest of us to see.

Believing for you,

Patsy

I stayed in constant contact with Carol, my friend of fifty years, as she marched through her difficult time, and may I say it was my pleasure and joy.

Yes, friends were meant to be part of God's resuscitation team. I often talk of friends because they are so precious. Don't miss the blessing out of fear of conflict or failure. People who insulate themselves against closeness and withdraw into solitary worlds will become mentally and emotionally rickety. Don't go there. Instead, take a deep breath and reach out as many times as it takes to find friends. I agree with Emily Dickinson, who said, "My friends are my estate."

Carol Update: Her hair has grown back. Although she was hoping for a lush crop, which she says she's never had, she's grateful for enough to fluff up and stay warm. The doctors believe they have eradicated the cancer and that she's free to do other things with her time, instead of flipping her wig for wee children and showing up for chemo. Thank you, Jesus.

10

Imagination Station

If you want to make an apple pie from scratch,
you must first create the universe.

— Carl Sagan —

"Naked Boy!" I heard a youth shout. Then my four-year-old grandson, Noah, appeared in my office doorway clad only in his Spiderman underwear, hands firmly planted on his hips.

"Hi, Nana, I'm Naked Boy," he stated proudly.

"Let me guess, Noah, are you a superhero?"

"Yes-s-s," he called back as he flew away, headed for the kitchen shouting, "Nak-ed Boy!"

What a way to begin a day, with a visitation from an imaginary hero, who, I'm grateful to say, doesn't comprehend the meaning of the word *naked*. Children help us to remember not to be stodgy.

Getting up in the wee hours to experience the first rays of light conquering darkness heartens me as well. I watch the ebony melt from the sky and drizzle behind the distant stand of trees, and my senses awaken. Those first morning moments when the sun seems to ignite a horizon of hope—a new dawn, a new day, a new beginning—who doesn't need that?

"And God saw the light, that it was good; and God divided the light from the darkness" (Genesis 1:4).

Yesterday can't be altered, tomorrow can't be predicted, and today can't be controlled any more than I can adjust the sun's path. While that could make us feel helpless, I find a deep comfort in the knowledge that the one who placed the sun on its course has lit a distinct path for us. The path is filled with purpose and with the potential for interior prosperity: "You will show me the path of life" (Psalm 16:11).

While on earth, we will encounter both darkness and light, but that will not always be so. A day will come when Christ in all his glory and light will fill every shaded nook and every shadowed cranny, and darkness will be no more. Nothing will be as we now know it, and earth and God's people will experience full redemption. Imagine that. Just imagine!

"There shall be no night there: They need no lamp nor light of the sun, for the Lord God gives them light" (Revelation 22:5).

I love that God gave us imagination. He knew we would need it to see beyond where we are to what might be. Certainly the dark enemy longs to corrupt the bright light of imagination; so we must put boundaries on where we allow our thoughts to go. Yet we must not ignore the gift of thinking beyond ourselves because that's how we explore creativity and hope.

When imagination is used to explore art, for instance, it can be enlightening. We tend to be boxy in our perspectives, but art can help us to take a leap into a bigger world. I believe in the emotionally healing value of creative endeavors. If you're one of those who say as I once did, "I'm not artistic," may I say unequivocally, "Oh, yes you are." Give yourself a chance to explore your creativity; risk making mistakes to find your undiscovered artist.

"There is nothing in a caterpillar that tells you it's going to be a butterfly," said Buckminster Fuller. You may not ever be lauded in an art museum, but your "brush strokes" might take place in the kitchen. Your soufflés may become fine enough to frame; your roast, a tender masterpiece of culinary genius. Your cupcakes, a cheery delight that adds sparkle to the neighborhood children's eyes. Or your herb-encrusted macaroni and cheese received by an elderly shut-in with eyes swimming with gratitude.

Perhaps you are a talented musician, jewelry designer, poet, tender caregiver, teacher, photographer, seamstress, hairdresser, inspired letter writer, or decorator. The list is limitless when it comes to all the ways art can be expressed.

When I was in Africa, women from the village gathered to present the Women of Faith team handmade gifts. Mine was a hollowed gourd used to carry milk for their babies. So simple yet so pretty, with its light beadwork and painted design. I treasure it. And they didn't just hand you your gift; they rejoiced with music and dance, then they gently drew you into their circle of celebration. Their brightly colored wraps and their warm smiles magnified the occasion. They were a living canvas painted with broad strokes of hospitality and generosity.

We have been made in God's *image* (from which the word *imagination* derives), and no one outdoes God's artistic flair, which is why people copy his art all the time. From a forsythia bush bursting with blooms, to a bowl of green apples, to clear vases of white tulips, they all drip with his creative involvement. Not to mention yonder mountain peaks, green-drenched valleys, and far off on the African savannahs, the acacia tree, a sentinel of beauty.

I just came in from my after-dinner walk, and I was delighted to view the beginning of God's Spring Collection. Daffodils, pansies, and even a deep-purple hyacinth greeted me. Now that's art. Art inspires, and inspiration beckons us to join in the creative process in all we do. "He has made everything beautiful in its time" (Ecclesiastes 3:11).

Color is paramount to art, and the wonderful thing about color is it can be splashed across all of life's offerings: our attitudes, our speech, our clothing, our gift giving, and our emotional lives.

Why are we so moved by a crimson sunset, an ocher-dappled masterpiece, and a fistful of fuchsia peonies? Have you ever become misty over a glorious musical arrangement, a stunning sunrise, or a stirring dramatic performance?

We are hardwired to respond emotionally to the wonder of art. I believe God has given us many elements in this life that help to heal us, inspire us, and remind us of our Creator, as well as enlarge our interior worlds. Art might well top the list of contributors to those benefits.

Do you have a favorite artist? (Mine is Winslow Homer.) What about a favorite classical piece? (Mine, *Canon in D*.) What flowers thrill your senses? (Gardenias, thank you.) When was the last time you walked through the woods? (November.) Have you handpicked a bouquet lately? (Roses . . . from Kroger . . . oops.) Or attended a play, ballet, or read a classic? (*Out of Africa*.) Have you in recent months walked on a beach, skipped rocks on a lake, or photographed a child (grandchildren), a pet (Cody, a Jack Russell terrier), or an elderly person (uh-oh, does my hubby count)?

These activities "spa" our senses, they mist our minds, and they contribute to our sensibilities. Sometimes unplugging from our routines and losing ourselves in life's art is the most healing thing we can do for our stretched-out emotions. That's why therapists use handcrafts in recovery programs, why doctors recommend vacations, and why folks escape to tents, cabins, mountains, boats, and camps. And often tucked in their backpacks are sketchpads, a Bible, a camera, and a journal. We seem to instinctively understand that we need art expressions.

We just know if we sit on a pier with a fishing line in the water we might snag a little sanity. Or if we sleep under the stars, we'll air out our musty minds. Or if we float across a rhythmic bay, we'll step back on land calmer and better prepared to handle the tidal waves of obligations on our desks. I personally love to get lost in a museum for a morning and then reflect on what I saw with a friend over blueberry muffins and hot tea.

Have you ever stepped inside a painting? In your imagination, I mean. Somehow curators don't appreciate our getting within spitting range of masterpieces, lest we whip out our paints and put mustaches on Rembrandt's maidens or sketch a vulture on the shoulder of Whistler's mother.

It's wonderful to find a painting you love and then to study it. Sit, observe it, and then ask yourself what you like about it: the subject matter, the color palette, the artist's style? Then mentally enter the picture and try to imagine what the artist was thinking, during what time of day you think the picture was painted, where the light source originates, what the people in it are doing, how you think they feel (tired, bored, joyful, in love). And before you leave the museum, visit the gift store and buy postcard-size pictures of your favorite paintings to refer to later.

Then, when you get home from your art tour, expand your experience by researching the artists you most appreciated. Just Google the artist's name and learn who inspired him or her and what struggles the artist faced. You might want to check online for Mary Cassatt, Pierre-Auguste Renoir, George Seurat, or Thomas Eakins. Or you may prefer Ansel Adams's black-and-white photography or the sculptures of Michelangelo or Gianlorenzo Bernini, and then there always are those who become ardent Pablo Picasso fans.

Find your interests and explore them. Not only will you broaden your mind, but also just think how impressed your friends will be when you casually drop into a conversation that you've been researching Hubert Gerhard's life-size bronze in Munich of the Archangel Michael slaying the devil. Or you've been studying a John Singer Sargent painting that hangs in the Museum of Fine Art in Boston. The work, done in 1882 when Sargent was only twenty-six years old, was entitled *The Daughters of Edward Darley Boit*. This painting caused a stir in Paris because of Sargent's unorthodox scattered positioning of the young sisters, which later proved to be sadly prophetic. (None of the four beautiful sisters married. Two by adult life suffered with mental illness and two remained close. Look at the painting to see if you can figure out which girls did what. And then ask yourself, "How did Sargent know?")

Trust me, critiquing art will be more inspiring and enriching than reiterating Simon's scathing reviews of last week's tryouts for *American Idol*. Creative expressions expand our thinking.

Don't be surprised if the artist inside you begins to rise up, wanting to be recognized. Luci Swindoll, my friend, coworker, artisan, and art mentor, taught me this type of personal exploration of paintings and lit a fire for art within me that I hope never goes out. I'm doing my utmost to fan that flame in my grandsons, who are showing artistic potential. Hanging at this moment in my home is the most dapper monster your eyes have ever seen, and he's guarding my kitchen from cookie thieves. I love that my six-year-old artist, Justin, signed it, which makes it far more valuable.

Noah continues to run artistically through the hallways of home, leaping tall buildings in his underwear. Naked Boy lives on. Hopefully Noah will retire this hero before adulthood and trade him in for, perhaps, a workbench and tools. As Pablo Picasso once remarked, "All children are artists. The problem is how to remain an artist once he grows up."

Perhaps your arty endeavors are best seen by the way you stir up the soil to cause riotous blooms to spring forth from the earth. You may be one of those garden architects who knows just where to tuck pools of petunias, fill a fence with morning glories, or array corners with ornamental peppers and fountain grass. "Green fingers are the extension of a verdant heart," said Russell Page.

Really, when you think of ways to revive your outlook, what's more medicinal on a temperate day than to spot a crowd of lilies of the valley nestled under a cherry tree or to be hypnotized by the rhythmic sway of hollyhocks nodding over a picket fence or to be left woozy from the intoxicating fragrances of roses and lilacs as you enter your backyard?

And how divine to follow a path and find you're ankle deep in lavender, with hydrangea blossoms encircling you. Being tucked among butterfly bushes, black-eyed Susans, and nests spilling over with black-capped chickadees is joyous.

Before we leave the garden, let's tarry a bit and watch the cardinals red-dash across sunflower palettes and dart between the deep-green needles of an evergreen. Oh, heart, be still.

When my mind runs out of creative ideas, just cozy me into a garden, and it not only will restore me, but it also will inspire my imagination to grow wider, deeper, sweeter, and grander. After all, as Mrs. C. W. Earle said, "Half the interest of a garden is the constant exercise of the imagination."

I leave the garden with fewer knots inside me. It's as if breathing in the atmosphere has allowed me to exhale some of my tension. The artistry of nature's beauty seems to replace the drab air that can cloud my thinking. Someone said, "You can bury a lot of problems digging in the dirt." Amen!

So what turns the crank on your imagination? Perhaps stimulating conversations do. I've found intentional chat sessions helpful to stretch my mind in problem solving. That's a healing form of art, for sure. When someone helps me to see beyond my stuck place, it paints my world with perspective.

Maybe you're a songwriter. My friend Ginger writes inspired worship music that her church uses at its women's retreats. Her joyful noise fills hearts with praise. What a holy exercise. And oh, how it pleases the Lord when we sing to him.

Perhaps you prefer to twirl your imagination wheel by teaching. We all applaud those who impart life-giving information with zeal. My pastor, Chuck Swindoll, is riveting. He makes learning a high calling. I have to wipe away tears during his sermons over the sheer privilege of hearing such a fine and imaginative orator.

Chuck spends countless hours every week in study. He is a consummate student and an accomplished man of letters, letters that spell a-r-t in all he does.

Now, what about us? What form of art makes our hearts skip a beat? Here's an idea: why don't you sign up for a class just outside your comfort zone? Maybe a cooking class, book club, stained-glass demonstration, writing seminar, or pottery or dulcimer lesson. Some of these only require an evening but could enhance and expand your creative repertoire and surprise you with your untapped potential. That's right, *you*.

And remember, artistic endeavors can be therapeutic to our uptight bundle of emotions. I find I can't talk about emotional recovery without exploring the topic of art; I try to tuck it in everything I write because I think it's crucial for our mental health.

If you're already overobligated, please don't join a class. Instead, take a nap. Really. Then, when you are well rested, figure out what you can do to thin your uptight-must-do list to make sane space for art. It will make you more ingenious, fun, textured, and more satisfied with your trek here on this wondrous, spinning kaleidoscope called God's green earth.

"So God created man in His own image; in the image of God He created him; male and female He created them . . . Then God saw everything that He had made, and indeed it was very good" (Genesis 1:27, 31).

11

Holy Post-Its

Who is more foolish, the child afraid of the dark
or the man afraid of the light?

— Maurice Freehill —

Have you ever read all 176 verses of Psalm 119? C'mon now, honestly? Every verse? If not, I dare you. In fact, I double dare you.

Here's why: those verses are like Post-it Note reminders for our zany emotions. But because it's such a cotton-pickin' long chapter, we're tempted to start reading but not finish.

Depending on the Bible translation you use, that psalm contains a number of different words that all mean "God's Word." They include *ordinances, testimonies, statutes, precepts, laws, promises, decrees,* and *commandments.*

About halfway through this psalm, you may think to yourself, *This is repetitious.* Exactly. It's meant to be. It's a way to secure our minds with the protective counsel offered in Scripture.

If you have had children or pets, you know how many times you have to repeat important instructions. ("If I've told you once, I've told you a hundred times: float your sailboat in the sink, not the commode!")

The psalmist (it's possible multiple writers contributed to this psalm) knows the benefit of repetition—line upon line. In its original Hebrew, Psalm 119 is an alphabetic acrostic, meaning its lines use each letter of the Hebrew alphabet in order. In addition to the clever, easy-to-remember structure, it is full of necessary reminders to keep us on the narrow yet lit path. Think of this long song as a symphony of truth, and then allow God's Spirit to sing it to your inner self. Since it's comprised of so many divisions, perhaps you might want to steep in it a section at a time.

Also I find keeping lists as I read helps me to retain and to learn. Now that I'm older than the gopher wood Noah used on the ark, I need notes to support my leaky brain. At last count I was three brain cells short of a vacancy sign . . . and I'm still in the youth of my old age.

Where was I? Oh, yes, the lists . . . from Psalm 119, I wrote down a few of the benefits for those who choose to make God's truths an integral part of their thinking. There are tons more.

1. *"I would not be ashamed"* (v. 6). That's an emotional biggy. Shame is a dark cloak of human misery that diminishes all light. We girls seem especially prone to shame's impact. Perhaps that's because we're more likely to be the abused. I'm thankful to say that, like a rose, if we are crushed, even our brokenness can rise up again as fragrance. "He raises the poor out of the dust, and lifts the needy out of the ash heap" (Psalm 113:7).

2. *"That I might not sin"* (v. 11). Any help I can get with my sinning is much appreciated—know what I mean? Why, I can't rise up in the morning and make my way to the mirror without some ungracious thought chirping in my mind. Let too many unexpected things happen

at the beginning of the day (doorbells, telephones, deliveries), and I can be downright ornery. Yes, I need the monitoring of the Word written in my being to help me steer clear of cantankerous tendencies.

3. *"I may see wondrous things from Your law"* (v. 18). I love the thrill of opening my Bible and reading a verse that flashes like a neon billboard of hope. God promises us through the psalmist that sort of intellectual unveiling when we passionately seek the Lord through his Word.

I'm not suggesting that every time I open my Bible I see clearly. Sometimes, after mulling over verses, I'll think, *I don't get it.* But I've found that if I continue daily to read and study, lights of understanding flicker on, and I not only begin to "get it," but also I'm aglow with revelation joy. It's sort of like when our eyes adjust in a dark room, and we recognize a party for us is about to be unveiled, and our loved ones are in attendance.

Speaking of loved ones, the Bible is all about our family tree, our "in-the-beginning" relatives. I know for sure I'm related to Moses. He started off his life as a basket case, for heaven's sake; of course we're kin!

But quite honestly I've been a Jonah as well. Like him I ran away and got in over my head. And I've certainly known a number of folks who would have relished the idea of throwing me overboard.

The Word is part of our heritage so that we might see that since Eden we've been in need of a Savior. God gives us his family, which deepens our connection with each other. Without fail when I study the Scriptures I find snapshots of myself in those who came before me. I have Eve tendencies and hide when I'm afraid, I have been a Naomi bitter with heartbreak, I have been an impetuous Peter with more words than sense . . . and I've been a Paul encountering Christ and experiencing a changed life.

The Bible is the best family album going.

Reading Scripture will help us to get a grip on our genealogy. Once we're adopted into God's family, we, like Ruth, can say, "Your people shall be my people" (Ruth 1:16).

4. *"For You shall enlarge my heart"* (v. 32). I'm afraid that if you were to measure my heart, at times it would be a narrow parcel, one that could be paced off quickly. I don't know about you, but I would like some holy acreage added to my little plot so that one would have to drive a Hummer for hours to survey it. My tendency to have a constricted perspective clouded at times by misinformation makes me an especially good candidate for this kind of heart expansion.

5. *"I will walk at liberty"* (v. 45). I believe that God helps us to deal with our elastic emotions as we integrate his counsel and walk in his ways. I find it appealing to have fewer knots inside me and, instead, to have more love. And love always leads to liberty.

6. *"This is my comfort in my affliction"* (v. 50). God's Word can enter into the fissures of our pain. He speaks life to us through his words. He gives us reason to keep on keeping on.

I remember when my only brother was killed in a car accident, I was inconsolable until a friend read to me, "I would have lost heart, unless I had believed that I would see the goodness of the LORD in the land of the living. Wait on the LORD; be of good courage, and He shall strengthen your heart; wait, I say, on the LORD!" (Psalm 27:13–14). Like a laser, the light of God's Word pierced through my grief to give me the courage to press on.

Those are just six benefits of being in God's Word; there are many more. I've barely skimmed the surface listed in just this psalm, but I wanted to kick-start your search for them.

When is the last time you got a swift kick in your intentions? It's scary when our Holy Post-It Notes start arriving by FedEx. Although for me, it usually takes a front-door delivery of hardships that smack me silly or sorrow that steals my breath or hurt that handles me roughly. How much better for us to store up truth now so that when the unexpected hits, we'll have protection and provisions. You'll never regret possessing a spiritual mending kit within you when your heart tears. To rummage about hither and yon in a panic leaves us vulnerable to the enemy's lie that we're hopelessly alone in our distresses. Satan always shows up when our protection is down. God's Word is our defense, our sword (Ephesians 6:17).

I also enjoy character studies. And, honey, a lot of lulus are in Scripture! I find that comforting. Yes, I admit that I'm Ms. Lulu herself. How puzzling that he who is holy loves us, and what a relief that our God is longsuffering toward us.

To pick a favorite Bible character would be more difficult than selecting a favorite Ben and Jerry's ice cream flavor. I could say Abigail because I admire her fortitude and resourcefulness, seen both in her difficult marriage and in her day of trouble. She left her fear on the pantry shelf, and in its place, she pulled down determination in the midst of imminent danger.

I could say Ruth because, as I donned sandals and walked with her from her homeland to Naomi's, I witnessed Ruth's devotion, strong work ethic, and humility. Ruth hung her cloak of sadness in her mother-in-law's closet and wrapped herself in a handmaiden's faith, and then she set about to make a better life for them both.

And I could say Deborah because of her success as a wise judge and a courageous leader. Listen, when people line up for your advice, that's saying something, and when the commander of the army refuses to go to war without you by his side, that's trumpeting your reliability. Deborah didn't fold under the pressure of so many people needing her, and she refused to take on the insecurities of others in the face of grave danger.

But my absolute favorite? Hmm, I'd have to say Moses. He floated into the Egyptian palace scene as a Jewish basket case. He grew up to become a criminal and soon found himself a fugitive herding sheep. Then, in the time it takes to set a bush afire, he traded in his dumb sheep for hundreds of thousands of hot-headed, whiny-breathed folks. Once the exchange was made, the hoopla began.

Yup, I love Moses. But I do think he should have had a GPS installed on his staff, because he showed strong signs of being like me, a directional dufus. Otherwise I don't think it would have taken him forty years to go a block and a half. Okay, okay, it was farther than that, but all things considered, not a lot. Gratefully God used the long way around to teach his people many lessons that they wouldn't have otherwise learned. That's God's heart for them and for us today, that he will use the path we are on for holy purposes regardless of how circuitous it may be. Perhaps that is why I love Moses' story best because it reminds me that even in the wilderness God will be a blazing presence.

Along the wilderness way, as I examined the Israelites' long, convoluted trek to the Promised Land, I found picnic baskets full of goodies on which my emotions could feast. I discovered them under palm trees, down wells, and atop mountains.

Examining the Israelites' actions often fed my need for direction in my life. And my "food" was actually a superior menu to the Israelites' fare, which was mostly wafer-thin rain bread. Think sweet saltines, but not as thick, no salt, and with a shelf life of zip. I think I might have held out for Twinkies. I hear their shelf life is just short of a millennium—

suited for wilderness wandering, and during war they could be lobbed at enemies like hand grenades. Twinkies are underrated.

When I study someone like Moses, I record tons of data as I research commentaries and await the Spirit's nudging me up one side of Mount Sinai and down the other with the old boy. Because, while I might be reading about some sandal-clad, hardheaded Israelite who refuses to follow the leader, it isn't long before I realize I'm also learning about rebellious, Reebok-clad me, who often is resistant to change.

Yes, Moses is my favorite, but I also must admit that I'm smitten with Gideon's story as well. Gideon is such an unlikely candidate for leadership, yet God chose to use a man who, when God arrived to appoint and anoint him, was actually hiding while he stomped out grain with his feet. Trust me, that isn't the way one threshes wheat. Oxen are employed, and it's done out in the open, but Gideon was so frightened by his enemies that he had taken up some unusual practices.

Having been housebound with fear, I know "unusual." We've been up close and personal for eons. For instance, see if you think this odd: some days I didn't fix dinner for my family, but I would bake half a dozen pies. Uh-huh. Or at the distant rumble of thunder, I would hide under the dining room table. And if I had to be in a car that was passing big trucks on the freeway, I would clench the dashboard in terror.

You see, when fear is dictating your actions, "bizarre" can become your norm. Imbalance becomes your scale. Survival drives you to the absurd. So Gideon and I . . . we be tribe mates.

Even Gideon's being an "unlikely" draws me to him because I identify. To say I had no credentials is to pad my résumé. We're talking zilch skill sets unless being manipulative and whiny counts. I guess I could have put on parties—pity parties were my specialty. But there's not a big market for those since most people prefer to have them alone.

When the angel of the Lord tells Gideon he is a mighty man of valor, Gideon throws a party—a big fat pity party. I told you I like this guy. He rattles off his résumé to God—actually, the lack thereof. Gideon informs God that he comes from the weakest of all the tribes and that he, Gideon, is the weakest of his kin. Don't you just know our omnipotent God was aghast? Not.

But I've done that indirectly, haven't you? When I've been asked to do something that feels outside my comfort zone, I recite all the reasons those making the request would be better off asking someone else. It's easy to use our emotions as the barometer of our capabilities. Not wise, just easy.

Oh yes, and Gideon complains about God's lack of availability. Now that, folks, was risky. Yet our God is patient with us, and Gideon proves that over and over again as he keeps asking God for proof the Lord will follow through with what he says.

I guess Gideon didn't know that "God is not a man, that he should lie; . . . hath he said, and shall he not do it?" (Numbers 23:19 KJV).

But God knows we are dust (Psalm 104:13), and dust bunnies need lots of emotional support. So God gives Gideon what he needs, and in addition, what he never expected. Gideon becomes a champion of the nation. Imagine that. He who once hid behind a tree and challenged God's identity and power became God's man of the hour, with Israel gathering under the shade of his leadership.

Gideon's story holds shade for our frayed self-esteems, our insecurities, our lack of credentials, and even for those moments when we wonder if God is there for us.

Scripture is crammed with insights, counsel, guidance, direction, and warnings meant to help us think God's way, which isn't natural for us, especially when we're in a tizzy.

Take, for example, Sarah of the Old Testament. When she didn't get pregnant in a timely fashion, she gave her servant girl Hagar to her husband so Hagar might "fill in" for what seemed to be God's oversight. Sarah had no idea what problems she would create in her world or ours when she chose to assist the Lord. It seemed reasonable to think at Sarah's age she wouldn't bear a child, which was her mistake. God isn't reasonable; in fact, often his ways are outrageous to our way of thinking. We'll never figure out God; he doesn't add up on paper. Not even a brilliant mathematician could get God to fit into a tidy column. He is not only deity but also holy mystery. He does, though, reveal parts of himself to us in Scripture, which is why we're admonished to search it diligently to be approved as one who need not be ashamed.

I'm certain that, had I been Sarah, I would have laughed, too, if I had heard I was to bear a child in my eighties. Honey, I'm in my sixties, and I can't carry my purse through the mall without setting off my osteoporosis, much less carry a baby in my wobbly womb. Imagine having hot flashes in between labor pains. Oh dear.

So I don't judge Sister Sarah. In fact, I get her. Bless her heart, she was doing her best work. And that's why we need the intervention of counsel . . . divine counsel. Left on our own, we're downright dangerous and often flat-out wrong.

So, in Deuteronomy the Lord instructed the Israelites regarding how they were to respond to God's counsel: "And these words which I command you today shall be in your heart; you shall teach them diligently to your children, and shall talk of them when you sit in your house, when you walk by the way, when you lie down, and when you rise up. You shall bind them as a sign on your hand, and they shall be as frontlets between your eyes. You shall write them on the doorposts of your house and on your gates" (Deuteronomy 6:6–9).

If I condensed those verses down for someone, I would suggest that person place God's Word like memos, first inside, then outside of herself. Memorize it. Study it. Sing it. Rehearse it. Teach it. It will do her well, and it will secure her people. (You got people? I got people, people I want to know his Word.)

Psalm 119 is a good starting place for Post-Its. Select your favorite verses and write them in your journal, pen them in calligraphy and frame them for your walls, tape them to your mirror, magnetize them to your fridge, and most importantly walk in the light they will add to your path.

Our emotions are in need of the nurturing elements of God's counsel, and we are in need of how to better manage our feelings so we don't jump ahead of the Lord's plan . . . or at least I am . . . Sister Sarah and me. Join us; you won't be sorry.

12

Becky's Bangles

Jewelry takes people's minds off your wrinkles.

⸾ Sonja Henie ⸾

Have you ever been left speechless? That hasn't been my tendency. In a talkative spurt, my verbiage could overflow a landfill. But when my sweet friend and coworker Sandi Patty stood on stage at a Women of Faith event to sing for sixteen thousand women and instead talked about me, I was baffled. I'm a fairly intuitive person and pick up vibes when something is about to go down. But I must say Sandi royally surprised me.

She said many generous and kind things about our year together sharing the Women of Faith Pre-Conference platform, at which she, Lisa Pierre, and I sang "Ain't No Mountain High Enough" (actually, I just did the speaking part, lest the audience sprint to the exits and hail cabs). Sandi announced that while she didn't have the power to bestow on me a degree of any type, she did have the ability to give me something else. I sat, mouth open, trying to figure out what was happening. Sandi then leaned down and extracted from a snazzy bag an award. Not just any award, but get this: Sandi gave me—tone-deaf, little wannabe-singer me—one of her very own Dove Awards that she had received for Female Vocalist of the Year.

I was speechless. I was honored. I was humbled (later I was helium-balloon proud). Imagine someone sharing her glory. The two-ton Dove statue (it really is heavy) sits on my fireplace mantel. I feel blessed to have experienced her lavish gesture of friendship and validation.

Did you ever wish you could bestow an honor on someone you feel deserves it?

My mom, Rebecca, should have been knighted, crowned, or at the very least received one rousing standing ovation by an Astrodome-size audience. She raised and endured three precocious children. Of course, we all know what they say about the apple that topples off the tree . . .

Actually, Mom is with Jesus now; so she doesn't need anything I could offer, but the longer I live the more I appreciate her efforts on our family's behalf. No doubt she was our family's superglue. Oh sure, she made her share of bloopers, but Mom did far more right than wrong, and her most impressive quality was that she never stopped chugging. If ever there was a little engine that could, it was this four-foot-ten-inch bundle of Southern determination.

Why does it take us so long to recognize others' sterling contributions? Truth be known, unlike her center-stage daughter, Mom wasn't drawn to large-scale attention. Mom and I differed in a number of ways, which often kept us at arm's length, trying to figure out each other. I loved an audience; she loved her privacy. I liked to be in the center of hubbub; she hugged the periphery and sought solace. I wanted to speak out; she wanted to sneak out.

Her seemingly "odd" behavior that once annoyed me now beckons me. Oh, I still love an audience, but now I, too, value my privacy. While I don't like missing out on life, someone else can put the hubs on bub; I'll just slip out early and catch up another day.

Yup, Mom had more right than I knew. I did applaud her personally while she was living, but she deserved more . . . much more.

When I was a young teen, my mom sold costume jewelry. Today, forty-eight years later, I still have many pieces that she collected. They aren't my taste, so I'm not sure why I've held on to them; perhaps to have the stimulus they offer my memory. I can still see Mom in my mind's eye proudly wearing different necklace sets and then carefully displaying the rest for customers. She did like pretty things.

Yet far more valuable to me is when I reach into my mind and pull up memories of her personage. Not so much how she looked or what she did, but more who she was. Today, and for many years now, I've drawn from Mom's life example for my own journey. She was a hard worker with a good sense of humor and a never-quit attitude. Mom loved the Lord, and she truly cared about others.

So I would like to leave you with these reminders on how to untangle your zany emotions that I'm going to call . . .

Becky's Bangles

How to Add Sparkle to Your Life
(or Five Helps with Your Rubber-Band Bundle)

Love the Lord

How does one love the Lord? It sounds good, but when our rubber bands start snapping, how do we hold true to that commitment?

One truth that has empowered me is understanding that I don't have to be taken hostage by my emotions. Christ gave his life for our liberty, our freedom from sin's dictatorship, as well as from our emotional turmoil. God designed our wills to be stronger than our feelings. We can keep our wills toned by refusing (with Christ's help) to give in to what's not healthy and honorable.

So that means the next time I'm ticked at my husband, instead of escaping into another room to nurse my hurt, I hold my ground, pray, lower my voice, pray, and calmly work through the conflict. Did I mention pray?

Or one might start an exercise program for willpower by refusing that luscious dessert everyone else is having, if for no other reason than to build up discipline. Denial can be character strengthening.

How is saying no to a caramel frap going to help us? It's funny (strange, not ha-ha) how refusing small things prepares us for more critical issues that require a "no" in our lives. This idea is based on the principle that, when we are faithful in little things, God will give us more. In this case that doesn't mean more dessert, sorry, but more resolve.

What does all that have to do with loving the Lord? I've found that when I offer up to God the imbalances in my life and apply his principles, my eyes are opened. I begin to see (heart enlightenment) why he gives us scriptural guidelines and counsel. And as my desire for his ways grows, my capacity to love him increases.

The Lord doesn't have to work on loving us; that's a done deal. It's we who emotionally vacillate and then wonder about his presence when times are tough, people are cruel, and hope is dim.

When I was a teen, I met another teenage girl whom I enjoyed hanging out with, except she had an annoying habit: she obeyed her mother. She even sought her mother's counsel. One day I asked her, "Do you always listen to your mom?"

"I didn't used to," she answered, "but then I ended up pregnant and had to give up my baby because I was so young. During that time I thought a lot about things my mom had said to me about my choices and the kids I ran around with, and I realized everything she had said was true. So to answer your question, yes, I do listen to my mom. I'd be foolish not to because she's lived longer than I have, and she knows what she's talking about."

At that stage of my life, I had no plans to listen to anyone; so I found this girl's answer tedious. Down the road of my rebellion I paid a big price to be stripped of that pride. I learned that God offered me truth, and I'd be foolish if I didn't receive it. He's been around a lot longer than I have, and he knows what he's talking about.

The more I study God's Word and spend time in prayer, the fuller my reservoir of truth is. Then, when I'm caught between a rock and a hard place, I can draw from that well. I don't have to flail about like one without hope. No doubt about it, the more I learn of him, the more I love him. You can't help but love the one who loves you and makes such provision for you.

Care About Others

"If you cannot do great things, do small things in a great way," said Napoleon Hill. My mom sure knew how to do that. She was a detail person with high standards, and while that could make her downright impossible to please, it also added flair and beauty to all she did. Whether she was addressing an envelope, icing a cake, pressing a shirt, or topping off a gift with a bow of her own making, Becky had style. She knew how to iron wrinkles into submission, scrub pans into brilliance, and force dying plants into new life. If you had dropped by our house, I promise you things would have been spiffy, and Mom would have communicated that your presence graced our home.

My dad was a milkman; so Mom had a limited income to work with to make our home hospitable. Yet somehow she made old things look new, inexpensive items appear fine, and common food garner applause from her guests.

I learned by osmosis from Mom that love covers a multitude of imperfections—ordinary food tastes better on a well-tended table; clean is as good as new; details add up and matter; and people respond to compassion.

I also learned the best therapy to help you over an emotional slump is to get up and do something for someone else.

Work Hard

Mom came from a family of do-it-yourselfers. She and her three sisters all looked forward to a day of productivity, but I wouldn't say they were workaholics, because they also knew how to sit a good chair. Usually, though, their hands were busy crocheting, knitting, making quilts, or snapping green beans.

They didn't hesitate to roll up their sleeves and glow from their efforts and later collapse in chairs with glasses of sweet tea. Close by the chairs were cardboard hand fans with wooden handles used to shoo away little gnatty critters and relieve the summer heat on their faces. They would talk, laugh, and rock their chairs while the smell of fresh-picked green beans simmered on the back of the stove. Soon they would move from the yard to the kitchen where they would make short work of the preparation for one of the best chicken and cornbread dinners you ever ate.

My mom was a strong model of a hard worker, but she was a

reluctant teacher. She would rather do it herself than hassle with a child who couldn't produce up to her high standard. It didn't take me long to learn that because I couldn't please her, I should let her do what needed to be done. Out of her desire to have things perfect and to keep peace, she let me slip out of the learning loop, and I grew up allowing others to carry my workload.

It's demeaning to wake up as a young adult and realize you're lazy. I discovered how hard it is to learn an industrious lifestyle once you are grown—not impossible, just hard. By God's grace and much effort, I've turned into a hard worker. In fact, now I have to watch that I don't tip in the other direction because I want to make up for lost time. In place of my slothful lifestyle is a strong sense of dignity and satisfaction. As I inched toward change, I often drew on Mom's demonstrated work ethic. She ended up being not only my model but also, indirectly, my teacher.

Never underestimate the impact of your family's offerings. You've learned more than you know. Trust me.

Laugh a Lot

Mark Twain once said, "Be careful of reading health books. You may die of a misprint." I loved to hear my mom chortle. Maybe because it meant she would be more amiable to my requests, or perhaps because she laughed so well. I could always tell when she was talking on the phone to her friend Bonnie because the sounds of Mom's laughter would skip down the halls of our home and fill the air with joy. Many times as a kid I would hear her laughter from another room. Even though I had no idea what was so funny, I would laugh too. It just seemed that when Mom laughed, the day was brighter and my heart was lighter.

Laughter is not only positive but also powerful. Along with being a magnet that draws others in, it serves as medication for our interior lives. That cancer wards incorporate laugh clinics into hospitals ought to tell us a great deal. And shared laughter makes even enemies friends, if only for a moment. Our world could use a good dose of friendly.

"The joy of the LORD is your strength" (Nehemiah 8:10). Now, I realize this verse is talking about a much deeper level of spiritual experience than just laughter, but I do believe laughter is a part of that joy. But I've bumped into some folks whom I thought laughed far too much. Their constant giggles felt like a nervous reaction instead of a spilling over of pleasantness. Tittering breeds an uneasiness in others because it doesn't feel authentic. It's like fear and insecurity are dressed up in a funny voice.

So we're back to the "balance" word. Honestly, I don't think we can discuss emotions without having to hit the balance button again and again. I promise you that in this topsy-turvy, inside-outside world, we won't be able to maintain balance, but it should always be our goal. And along the journey let's take time to chortle every day. It will smooth out some of the bumps in the road and help others up steep inclines.

Never Give Up

Author Dave Barry says, "Nobody cares if you can't dance well. Just get up and dance." The grit of David. The persistence of Ruth. The bravery of Daniel. The decisiveness of Deborah. The fortitude of Joseph. The dedication of Joshua. The perseverance of Jacob. The tenacity of the woman with the issue of blood. The doggedness of Paul.

Never give up.

We have examples: they crowd Scripture's pages. They reside in our neighborhoods. They work at care facilities. They struggle in rehab centers. They guide their wheelchairs through crowded streets. They take school courses in their jail cells. They weep in support groups. They live in our homes.

Never give up.

Les has had three heart attacks, is a brittle diabetic, has extensive neuropathy complications, and also has arthritis. He is warm, kind, and very funny. He makes people laugh every day.

Never give up.

I met a woman recently who had been married fifty-nine years. They never gave up.

My friend has lost the use of her right hand. She can no longer play piano or tennis, garden or draw. So she visits the sick; she does decorating consultations, invests in her grandchildren, and teaches herself new skills with her *left* hand.

Never give up.

A dear friend had a public moral failure, a marriage collapse, and battled depression. Today, after accountability restoration and emotional counseling, she offers hope to others who are trying to make a fresh start.

Never give up.

I don't know what has your rubber-band emotions in knots today, but I do know that God is still in the resurrection business. And while others may judge us, Christ waits with open arms to restore our dignity and guide us to a higher path.

Never, ever give up!

So those are Becky's Bangles. I hope they help to guide you to untangling your zany emotions as much as they have me. Way to go, Mom; you've shown us a brighter and better path to travel by treading it before us.

13

Emmaus Road

Promise me you'll always remember: you're braver than you believe, and stronger than you seem, and smarter than you think.

— Christopher Robin to Winnie the Pooh —

As we continue on our journeys, each of us on an individual path, my prayer is that we will recognize Jesus when he comes to walk alongside us. Unlike his disciples who were trudging along on the road to Emmaus but didn't know the resurrected Jesus was traveling with them, may we listen studiously and take notes as he explains to us some of life's complexities. He does that for us through his Word, his Spirit, his people, and his creation.

Along our way we mustn't allow our sorrows to disable us, but instead we must filter them through God's plan and mercies, which will add depth to our heart's content.

My longtime friend and the chaplain for Women of Faith, Lana Bateman, often reminds me, "The sign of true maturity in a life is when joy and sorrow walk hand in hand."

God made us gals emotionally wealthy, giving us the potential to be prosperous in our dispositions and intuitions. We all have regrets, but we must learn to receive what Christ offers freely: forgiveness. And we must realize that Jesus redeems our failures for his divine purposes. I can't explain that kind of love, but I am a recipient. Lana also says, "Sovereignty is the salvation of regret." What a relief to know that God's established plans from the beginning of time cannot be interfered with by my mistakes. His holy purposes are not hampered by our failures. He will accomplish and complete his work. The Lord longs to give us a full life with an array of emotions that enhance our faith. He will take our rubber-band bundle and make sense of it. He will give us definition, he will guide us toward resolution, and he provides us the hope of a divine destination. But it's a process, so don't be discouraged. It's an Emmaus Road of ongoing revelation.

Expect life to be joyful and rugged. Let's be wise enough to lean into what comes our way. If God has allowed it, it comes with purposes we may not understand . . . yet. "Rain! Whose soft architectural hands have power to cut stones, and chisel to shapes of grandeur the very mountains," said Henry Ward Beecher.

Pack up your rubber bands and follow the narrow road; it leads to the widest joy. Along the way, enjoy your rich emotional design.

Welcome to the Study Guide

C'mon in and allow me to welcome you to the hospitable study guide. This is where we take what we've read with our eyes and help make it more a part of how we see with our heart, mind, and spirit. Thoughtfully flipping through the pages of a book can be such a rich experience. It can shape our thoughts and emotions. It can draw us closer to God and a truer understanding of ourselves. The intention of this study guide is to provide a natural gateway from the book into direct engagement and life-changing moments with the Father . . . with laughter and fun all the way there. Our Father delights when we splash around in joy. So, as we go through the study guide chapters, please revisit the book chapters and use the DVD clips to giggle, and inspire deep thoughts as well as understand our true feelings. The end result, I hope, will be a renewed sense of closeness with the one who cares for us and a new sense of understanding those zany emotions that have been a part of God's great design for us all these years. Before you go on, though, remember: this is your time with God. There is so much of him to experience. Trust him to walk with you through the material, to be your Partner, and lean on him to gain a new understanding of your heart. And never, never, never stop having fun as you do.

Contain Yourself

Our Goal Today: To get in touch with the ways we are affected by our emotions and to make a plan to let God work with us in areas where we need improvement.

Scripture to Ponder: Romans 12:2

When it comes to your emotions, which of the following animals best describes you and why?

- ❍ an angry lion because ______________________________.
- ❍ a hissing snake because ______________________________.
- ❍ a barking dog because ______________________________.
- ❍ a tiny kitten because ______________________________.
- ❍ a playful otter because ______________________________.

What are some of the things that regularly press your emotional buttons?

How do you feel after you've had an emotional meltdown?

- ❍ vindicated
- ❍ embarrassed
- ❍ justified
- ❍ mortified
- ❍ other: ______________________________

How do the people around you respond to your emotional meltdowns?

- ❍ they're just like me
- ❍ they steer clear until the dust settles
- ❍ I dare them to respond
- ❍ I don't have emotional swings

Emotions can do two things: they can get you tapped into the way God beautifully made you or they can make people wonder if we really know God! Consider your emotional episodes. What do they say about you?

What do they say about God?

Maybe you're happy with your responses above; maybe not. This study is about helping you untangle those troublesome emotions. It's about finding those places where your emotions hide and exposing them to God's grace. But it's not about you locking away your emotions so that they'll never be seen again. Refusing to deal with your emotions can be as harmful as being too emotional.

What are some of the containers in which your emotions are kept?

- ❍ snappy answers
- ❍ sarcasm
- ❍ overreaction
- ❍ passive-aggressive behavior
- ❍ pouting
- ❍ outbursts
- ❍ cynicism

Review the list again from the perspective of your loved ones. Would they answer this question about you differently? If so, how can you explain the difference in the perceptions?

One of the most debilitating emotions is anger. We all deal with things that make us angry, yet we often fail to deal adequately with our anger. What are some recent situations in which you have become angry?

Was your anger directed at a person or a situation?

View the "Rubber Bands" video clip. In what ways are your emotions similar to those described in the video? Do you feel like a knotted wad of rubber bands sometimes?

What determines the quality of your life?

- ❍ your emotions
- ❍ your relationship with Christ

In the same way that our negative emotions can control our lives, our positive emotions have the same power. In many situations, our emotions battle for control. It's the classic good-versus-bad encounter. Think about the tug-of-war between your positive and negative emotions. Which one wins most of the battles and why?

View "Please Everybody." What does this clip say to you? How can you apply it to your life?

Take a Moment to Untangle

List in the space below three desired results from this study. At the end of the study, review the list to see if you got what you were looking for. Take a few moments and pray, asking God to open your eyes and ears so that you might see and hear his love for you. Then let his love transform your life. Read and commit to memory Romans 12:2, and let it become your theme verse for this study.

In Romans 12, Paul instructed the Romans (and us) to give their lives to God. Paul didn't mean just your initial salvation. He meant to continue to give their lives to God. It's funny how we offer ourselves to God and then pick up the offering and take it home again. If you don't remind yourself that you belong to God, you'll forget and that's when things can get out of hand. When God isn't in control of your life, you are.

Is God really in control of your life? If so, write a prayer of thanksgiving in which you express how he affects your every action. If not, write a prayer asking God to take total control of your life and your emotions. Every time you pick up this book, reread the prayer and thank God for what he is doing in your life.

Chapter One

Pierced Years

Our Goal Today: To discover the intimacy and peace that come from living in God's secret place.

Scripture to Ponder: Psalm 91:1–16

View "Air Force." What are some ways in which God has sustained you through something you thought was unbearable?

Describe the last time you experienced a "woe is me" moment. What happened to cause this experience?

What was the spiritual effect of the "woe is me" experience?

- ❍ it had no spiritual effect
- ❍ it affected me for a moment
- ❍ it affected me for a long time
- ❍ I'm still not over it

Read Psalm 91:1–16. The psalmist refers to dwelling in God's "secret place" as a good thing (v. 1). The New International Version calls the secret place "the shelter." We get the idea that being near to God is a place of safety and security. Sometimes we are threatened from the outside. But sometimes the biggest threat to our safety and security is internal—a lack of self-esteem, for instance.

Self-esteem is defined as "a sense of one's own value." What are some things that positively or negatively affect your perception of your value? (Check all that apply.)

- ❍ the way I look
- ❍ what I perceive others think of me
- ❍ my socioeconomic status
- ❍ my friends
- ❍ my education and/or professional status
- ❍ the behavior of my children
- ❍ my spiritual relationship with God and other people
- ❍ other: ______________________________________

When you are feeling insecure, how do you usually respond?

Take a look at Psalm 91:2. Does this verse describe your response when you face fears or doubts? Why or why not?

Read Psalm 91:3–13. Why does God provide such safety and security for his people?

What keeps you from experiencing that safety and security?

What are your "hiding places"? Describe a couple of physical places.

Do you have the same view of yourself as God does? Why or why not?

Use the following scale to evaluate your degree of security:

insecure |————————————————| totally secure in God

Read Psalm 91:14–16. Once we meet the condition of verse 14, God promises to do certain things. In the space provided below, list the things God promises in verses 15–16.

Do the goals of your life include the things listed above, or are you seeking something that God never promises? Are you seeking what really matters to God or what really matters to you? The ultimate boost to your self-esteem comes when you totally submit yourself to God's purposes. That's when you'll discover the calmness that comes from living in God's secret place.

View "Grandson." What is the source of your joy in life?

How have you responded when someone has abandoned or fired you?

What happens when you've made one of those people the source of your joy?

Take a Moment to Untangle

Write a prayer that expresses your desire in response to this lesson. Begin each day with this prayer, asking God to take you into his secret place so that you can experience life the way he intended it.

Chapter Two

Nervous Nellie

Our goal today: To discover God's comfort in times of fear and look for ways to let God's presence overwhelm your fears.

Scripture to Ponder: 2 Timothy 1:3–12

Play "Faith and Fear." What fears are you facing right now?

To what degree are your fears interfering with your day-to-day life?

❍ not at all; I have no fears
❍ a little; my fears are real but manageable
❍ a lot; my fears seem to follow me everywhere I go
❍ I'm paralyzed by my fears

What are three boundaries you can establish to protect your mind and imagination?

1.
2.
3.

Consider your emotions. In the space provided below, list the positive and negative aspects of your emotions. Then list how your emotions affect those you love.

Positive Effects	Negative Effects

View "The Qualifier." Read 2 Timothy 1:1–12. While facing execution in a Roman prison, Paul wrote his final instructions to the young pastor, Timothy. Paul wanted to see Timothy, but he also wanted to make sure Timothy received final words of encouragement. Timothy was like a son to Paul, so he had some things he wanted to be sure to share with Timothy.

Timothy's faith had been nurtured by his mother (Lois) and his grandmother (Eunice). Paul recognized that Timothy's spiritual strength was built on a foundation laid by these two godly women.

For whom are you laying a godly foundation?

If Paul wrote to the person or persons listed above about your spiritual effect, what would he say?

Read 2 Timothy 1:6–7. Like many people, Timothy's spiritual fire diminished. Timothy was in a difficult situation. He faced some challenges that called for him to be bold and courageous. But the enemy of courage is fear. That's why Paul wrote the words in verse 7. Rewrite that verse in your own words as if Paul were writing it to you right now.

In verse 7, Paul identifies the antidote to fear. What is that antidote?

- ❍ determination
- ❍ God
- ❍ intelligence
- ❍ relationships
- ❍ other: ______________________________

In this verse, we see four principles that can help us overcome our fears:

Turn on the light of God's Word. How much time do you spend in Bible study each week?

The ultimate power for overcoming fear rests in the strength of our relationship with God, and our relationship with God is a direct result of the time we spend with him and in his Word. You will never overcome fear unless you invest time in developing and maintaining your relationship with the Creator.

Turn on the light of faith. Faith is what carries us from the known into the unknown. If we never make that journey, it says something about our faith (or lack of faith). When was the last time you stepped out on faith?

What was the end result of that experience? How did it affect you? How did it affect other people?

Turn on the light of your mind. Some people say that seeing is believing. Yet, faith says believing is seeing. As we believe, God allows us to see things we never would have seen apart from our faith in him. We miss out on tremendous joy because we fail to embrace God's vision. What is something that God is showing you right now?

What do you plan to do about the vision above?

- ❍ nothing, I'm scared
- ❍ wait for someone else to do it
- ❍ try to convince someone else to do it
- ❍ step out in faith and trust God's guidance

Turn on the light of friendship. We all need like-minded friends to support us through our times of uncertainty and uneasiness. Who are those people to whom you turn for support?

For whom are you a source of support?

Fear has a way of motivating some people and paralyzing others. This isn't the way God intended it to be. Take a look at 2 Timothy 1:8–12.

In this passage, Paul points out some of the things that could have happened to Timothy if he had let his fear overcome his faith. Is fear causing any of the following in your life?

- ❍ I don't talk about God like I should (v. 8).
- ❍ I'm more concerned about my comfort than being bold for God (v. 8).
- ❍ I am not living out God's calling in my life (v. 9).
- ❍ I am not being a positive spiritual force (v. 10).
- ❍ I am looking to be served rather than serving others for God (v. 11).
- ❍ I am afraid of suffering for the cause of Christ (v. 12).

Take a Moment to Untangle

Read 1 Timothy 3:12. Knowing God is different than knowing about God. Being persuaded means something more than wishful thinking. Only as we know him can we become persuaded. Which statement below is true about you?

- ❍ I know whom I have believed and am persuaded that he is able to keep what I have committed to him until that day.
- ❍ I know *about* God and am *hopeful* that he is stronger than the fears I face.

Pray asking God to make his presence in your life stronger than the fears you face.

Chapter Three

Ire Fire

Our Goal Today: To discover God's comfort in times of fear and to trust God to see you through.

Scripture to Ponder: 2 Timothy 1:3–12

View "Airport." What are three things that make you angry?

1.
2.
3.

When you get angry, how do you respond?

- ❍ I lose control and clean up the mess when I've calmed down
- ❍ I sulk and refuse to talk
- ❍ I blame someone else for making me angry
- ❍ I turn to God and seek His wisdom
- ❍ other:______________________________

What circumstances in life make anger beneficial?

Think about your overall attitude toward life. Where are you on the scale below?

Constant kindness |————————————| Constant anger

What does the attitude of your life say to others about your relationship with God?

- ❍ my life supports what I claim to believe
- ❍ my life contradicts what I claim to believe

How would you describe the relationship between kindness and truth?

In chapter 3, it says: "Kindness is a way to express feelings that's more likely to be heard by others because it takes the *attack* out of truth. It also tests our motives, because being kind is very hard when we're bent on revenge."

Have you ever been "bent on revenge"? What did you do? And what was the outcome?

Did you temper your response with kindness? Why or why not?

When truth is given in kindness, the resulting conversation can be honest and constructive. However, when kindness prevents us from telling the truth, the conversation accomplishes less because we over-look the way things really are.

Describe a time when your emotions or behavior got your faith in tangles.

What happened in the short term as a result?

What happened in the long term?

Think about your angry emotions. In what ways is anger affecting your . . .

appearance?
health?

sanity?
relationships?

Read 2 Peter 1:2–9. We really haven't learned until the knowledge penetrates our attitudes and actions. That was the message Peter presented to the early church. Some people had disconnected their faith from their everyday lives. They had compartmentalized their relationship with God. It was easy to play the part when necessary, but it wasn't necessary to play the part all the time. This inconsistency in spiritual behavior was confusing to nonbelievers. It's still confusing today!

Faith grows in fertile soil, and Peter describes that soil in 2 Peter 1:5–7. Read the passage and reflect on those attributes.

When you review the Scripture passage, you can see that kindness is a by-product of several other things—virtue, knowledge, self-control, perseverance, and godliness. It also is foundational to our ability to express godly love.

Let's go back and reconsider the characteristics in the list. In the space provided, define each term.

Virtue:
Knowledge:
Self-control:
Perseverance:
Godliness:
Love:

The Bible defines virtue as "Christlike character." How can believers discover and develop Christlike character in their emotional lives?

Reread your response. What things could you change in your emotional life when you consider what you've written?

Knowledge is really the practical knowledge of godly principles. How can believers discover godly principles?

In what areas of life is it most difficult to employ godly principles?
Self-control is the ability to control one's emotions rather than being controlled by them. Is it difficult for you to control your emotions? Why or why not?

Perseverance is the ability to use one's self-control to defeat and overcome temptation. What temptations are most bothersome to you?

What is the role of the Holy Spirit in defeating those temptations?

Godliness entails the concept of staying in close communication with God. In what ways do you maintain your communication with God? What are some things you can do to improve your communication with God?

Kindness is closely linked to godliness in that it is the application of godliness to earthly relationships. In what relationships do you need to exhibit more kindness?

What are three things you can do to become more like God in your attitude toward others?

Love, in this passage, is God's kind of love. It originates in the source of the love and is not conditional. God loves us because he is love; he can't be anything else. Love seeks the highest good for the object of the love. In what ways are you seeking the good of those you claim to love?

Take a Moment to Untangle

Take a good look at the way you perceive your personality and the way God perceives it. Are you pursuing Christlikeness in the way you interact with others? No one can do this perfectly—no one, that is, except Jesus.

List three areas where you could become more like Christ toward others.

1.
2.
3.

Pray asking God to give you wisdom to control your emotions when you are in situations that might be emotionally challenging.

Chapter Four

Perils of Pauline

Our Goal Today: To understand and embrace God's power to help you overcome the effects of self-pity in your everyday life.

Scripture to Ponder: Ruth 4:1–12

View "Piano Player." In what areas of life are you "determined" to have things your way?

When was the last time you had a good, old-fashioned pity party?

What caused you to feel sorry for yourself?

How do you feel when you've played the role of "damsel in distress" and gotten your way?

- ❍ I feel as if I won the battle and got what I was entitled to
- ❍ I feel as if I manipulated someone, but I don't feel guilty
- ❍ I feel guilty almost immediately
- ❍ I've never played the role

Self-pity is emotional quicksand. There is a moment when our personal feelings cross from being informative to being poisonous. This is when self-pity kicks in.

Think about a situation you are facing right now. In the space provided below, list your feelings and the results of those feelings. For instance, "I feel angry, so I will never speak to her again unless she apologizes."

Feeling	so I	Action

Review your feelings. Which of the feelings are positive? Mark them with a +. Which are negative? Mark them with a –. Review your actions. Which of them require someone else to do something? Mark them with an O. Which of the actions are totally dependent on you? Mark them with an M.

What do you discover in the exercise above? Based on this one situation, you can see if you are having positive or negative feelings. You also can see if you are putting the responsibility for solving the problem on the shoulders of someone else or on yourself.

Review your responses above. Do your feelings and actions lead to a solution or expand the problem?

Are you tangled in self-pity? If so, do you enjoy it?

How do you feel when someone whines to you?

- ❍ I want to listen intently.
- ❍ I want to out-whine him or her.
- ❍ I want to change the subject.
- ❍ I run and hide before it starts.

When it comes to self-pity, where are you on the scale below? (Mark the line with an X.)

Never experience it |————————————————| Addicted to it

When you are overcome with self-pity or have a habit of whining, there are a few things you need to do.

Take ownership. Admit that you are feeling sorry for yourself. As long as you deny it, you will never stop doing it.

Write your admission regarding the last time you dealt with self-pity.

Seek forgiveness. Feeling sorry for yourself is a telltale sign that you need to pause and consider God. If your faith is in him, you know that he is bigger than any situation you face. When we feel self-pity, we must turn to God and confess our lack of faith, asking for forgiveness.

In your most recent self-pity experience, why did your personal desires overshadow your faith?

What can you do to prevent that from happening in the future?

Recall God's Word. Several Scripture verses remind us of God's presence even in our most trying times. Try memorizing Philippians 1:21 and recite it each time you feel yourself cornered by self-pity.

List two or three friends you can call when you are feeling sorry for yourself. Chose those who will listen but won't let you indulge. Reach out to them and ask if they would be a "pity pal." Share with them how you're working on this area of your life.

Whose "pity pal" list should you be on?

One of the things that helps overcome habitual whining is the decision to praise God. Stop for a moment and list three things in your life for which God deserves praise.

1.

2.

3.

How did expressing that praise affect your attitude?

❍ positively . . . I feel better!

❍ negatively . . . I feel worse!

❍ none . . . I feel the same!

The book of Ruth is one of only two books in the Bible named for a woman. It presents a heartwarming story of love, loyalty, and redemption. Through her relationship with her mother-in-law, Naomi, Ruth learned about God's love and became a believer. Ruth was blessed in that she is in the family line of King David and, ultimately, Jesus Christ.

Read Ruth 4:1–12. By the time we get to the end of the story, Ruth has proven her commitment to Naomi and to Boaz. Understanding the events in chapter 4 requires a little basic knowledge about the cultural practice of redemption. Close relatives had the responsibility and opportunity to purchase the land of a family member if that land had been sold due to poverty. This had been the case regarding the land that had belonged to Naomi's husband, Elimelech.

Business usually was conducted at the city gate in the presence of the elders. This provided the formal background for the discussion between Boaz and the other family member. Because the other family member was more closely related to Elimelech, he had first choice to redeem the land—that is to buy it back from the one who purchased it when it was sold due to poverty. The other family member initially planned to buy the land, but when he was told that he also got Ruth as a wife in the deal, he backed out. This left the option to Boaz. He quickly exercised the option and redeemed the land, taking Ruth as his wife in the process.

As you read Ruth's story, what are some of the reasons Ruth could have felt sorry for herself?

What are some of the reasons you feel sorry for yourself?

In the end, Ruth was redeemed and used by God to bring to the world the ancestors of David and Jesus. Ruth rose above her situation and embraced life God's way.

View "Two Extremes." What is the danger of the two extremes mentioned in the video?

Like Ruth, you are valuable to God and the world. Through you, God wants to do things you never imagined possible. The choice is yours—RSVP to a pity party of one or decline the invitation through God's strength.

Take a Moment to Untangle

View "Unlikely Strength." Pray asking God to give you the strength you need to rise above your feelings of self-pity so that you can become all the he intends you to be.

Chapter Five

Infinity Pool

Our Goal Today: To recapture the life-changing joy that comes from the hope our relationship with God gives us.

Scripture to Ponder: John 11:1–44

How do you define hope?

What are some things that have provided you with hope in the midst of troubling situations?

View "God-given Opportunity." What are some things you would do if your qualifications were not an issue?

Where are you on the following scale?

Permanent hopelessness |————————————| Eternal hope

Albert Einstein said, "There are two ways to live your life. One is as though *nothing* is a miracle. The other is as though *everything* is a miracle."

Which statement do you feel is more true for you?

- ❍ Nothing is a miracle.
- ❍ Everything is a miracle.

What does your response reveal about your view of God?

On page 37, there are several statements describing what hope is. Reflect on those statements and then write a few statements of your own.

Hope is . . .
Hope is . . .
Hope is . . .

Hope isn't something we possess; it is an attitude of life.

View "Your Calling." In what ways has your calling been identified through . . .

validation?

open doors?

As you read Helen Keller's story, were you reminded of a time when you gave up on someone or when you were given up on by someone else? If so, what were you thinking and feeling during that time?

The search for hope leads us from situation to situation, doctor to doctor, church to church, job to job, even relationship to relationship. In what areas of life are you searching for hope?

- ❍ family
- ❍ career
- ❍ relationships
- ❍ spiritual
- ❍ financial
- ❍ physical
- ❍ emotional
- ❍ other: ____________________________

What are some things you do in your efforts to discover hope?

Read John 11:1–44. In this story, Mary and Martha had every reason to lose hope. Their brother, Lazarus, was sick and eventually died. What they wanted to happen—Jesus' arrival and subsequent healing of Lazarus—didn't happen.

Read John 11:21, 24. Describe Martha's condition.

Have you ever transferred your hope from the present to the future? If so, what was the situation you were facing?

Mary and Martha knew enough about Jesus to make them believe that he could have intervened prior to the death of Lazarus, yet they lacked the faith to believe that he could intervene after Lazarus died. How often does your faith get overwhelmed by your rational mind?

- ❍ it never happens to me
- ❍ it sometimes happens to me
- ❍ it always happens to me

Is the following statement true of you? "I have hope as long as I understand how the situation will work out." ______ true ______ untrue

How do you think Mary and Martha felt when Jesus called Lazarus from the tomb and Lazarus walked out?

Describe a time when your faith has been matured through a seemingly impossible experience.

How does that experience influence your faith today?

- ❍ it has no bearing because today's situations are different
- ❍ it reminds me that God is bigger and more powerful than anything I face

Your response to the question reveals your degree of hope. Hope reminds us that God has been with us in the past and will be with us in the future. Hope sustains us when the chips are down. Hope allows us to rise above the challenges of life so that God, not us, will be revealed to a doubting world.

Take a Moment to Untangle

Pray asking God to renew his presence in your life so that you can be an example of someone living with hope. Ask God to show you how he can use your responses to the situations you face to encourage someone who is going through something similar. Then ask God to make you aware of times when you play the role of damsel in distress and commit yourself to rising above that temptation.

Chapter Six

Chunky Monkey

Our Goal Today: To become the kind of woman who isn't driven by physical desires but rather by the desires to please your loving heavenly Father.

Scripture to Ponder: 1 Samuel 25:2–42

View "The Pink Harley." In what areas of life do you need the most godly restraint?

When it comes to your physical desires, what things cause you the most problems?

- ❍ food
- ❍ television
- ❍ socializing
- ❍ finances
- ❍ relationships
- ❍ shopping
- ❍ other: ______________________________

View "The Comforter." What have been some of the turning points in your emotional life?

When faced with one or more of the temptations above, what is your success rate in avoiding them?

- ❍ 0–25%
- ❍ 26–50%
- ❍ 51–75%
- ❍ 76–99%
- ❍ 100%

Do you often comfort yourself with food? If so, describe the sequence of events that leads you to indulgence.

If not, how do you deal with the physical effects of stress?

Do you believe that the way in which you deal with stress is helpful or harmful to your overall well-being? Explain your response.

View "Setting the Example." What is the pattern of your life?

- ❍ a biblical pattern
- ❍ an emotional pattern
- ❍ I'm not using a pattern

Read Romans 13:14. Are you obedient or disobedient to this biblical instruction? Write out your honest response.

When it comes to your eating habits, how healthy are they?

- ❍ I'm all-natural and fat-free
- ❍ I try to eat healthy, but just can't do it consistently
- ❍ I would eat whole-wheat Krispy Kremes if they made them
- ❍ if it doesn't clog arteries, it's not on my diet

View "Are You Ready?" Read 1 Samuel 25:2–42. Let's set the scene. Nabal was married to Abigail. Nabal was not the kindest or most humble person around. Matter of fact, he was downright mean and egotistical. Abigail was the moral strength of the family. She also was a faithful wife. As bad as Nabal was, Abigail was committed to the relationship. She had to endure his bad temper and his disregard for anyone other than himself. Abigail did the right thing because she didn't get distracted by the other pressures of life.

The story goes like this: David and his men were in the area in which Nabal owned land and raised sheep. David sent some men to Nabal and reminded him that David's men had been kind to Nabal's servants. They then asked for some provisions for David.

Nabal wasn't impressed. He didn't know David and refused to share with him. When the men returned to David, the situation got worse. David ordered his men to get their swords and prepare for battle. He assembled four hundred men to assist him in obtaining provisions from Nabal.

Nabal's servants warned Abigail that Nabal's rudeness had met its match. She gathered some bread, wine, meat, grain, raisin cakes, and other food items and went out to head off David's army. She pleaded with David not to seek revenge on Nabal. She agreed that Nabal had been foolish, but she pleaded for David not to do any harm to the innocent bystanders.

Abigail's honor saved the lives of several people that day. In what way is God using you for the benefit of others?

Abigail was prepared for an emergency. She knew what to do. How prepared are you for life's unexpected opportunities?

❍ I'm as prepared as Abigail was.
❍ I tend to try to figure out what to do while dealing with the problem.
❍ I fall apart and then clean up the mess later.

What enabled Abigail to do the right thing? What enables you to do the right thing?

Abigail had some specific qualities. How strong are you in each of these areas? (Mark each line with an X.)

	Weak	Average	Above Average
Dignity			
Discernment			
Intelligence			
Self-control			
Preparedness			
Fortitude			
Patience			
Humility			

Take a Moment to Untangle

View "Newlyweds." What are some things that cause you to turn to God?

Pray asking God to make you more and more like Abigail and less concerned about the things of this world. Begin by identifying three things you will do when your thoughts take you away from God and toward self-indulgence.

1.
2.
3.

Now spend time searching Scripture for verses to memorize that will encourage you in these areas.

Chapter Seven

Shoe Goo

Our Goal Today: To overcome our occasional moodiness by choosing to focus on the positives that come from our relationship with our heavenly Father.

Scripture to Ponder: Psalm 16:1–11

View "Pantyhose." What is something you've done to embarrass or humiliate yourself?

Where are you on the following scale?

Despair————————————————Enthusiasm

When you are tempted to journey down into the dumps, what do you do?

- ❍ fight it and win
- ❍ fight it for a while and then give up
- ❍ go along for the ride

- ❍ I'm never tempted to journey down into the dumps (think again!)

Describe the last time you were down in the dumps.

View "New Brakes." Now, using the following steps, describe how you could have responded differently to that situation.

1. *Recognize your choices*. You can't always choose how you feel, but you can choose how you respond. In the situation above, what were your response choices?

Why did you choose to let your emotions bottom out?

2. *Know yourself*. When you are tempted to be gloomy, to whom do you usually turn?

Is that person effective in helping you kick the gloom habit? If not, can you really say that your desire is to change your mood? Explain your response.

3. *Enlist a prayer partner*. One of the best defenses against bad moods is the wisdom that can be shared by a like-minded believer. Who is your prayer partner? ___________________________________

How could that person have helped you in the situation described above?

4. *Watch what you watch*. For the next few days, keep a journal listing all of the television shows and movies you watch. Go back and mark each as being encouraging or discouraging. Do the same with the music you listen to. Then go back and evaluate those external influences. Are you being affected positively or negatively by your entertainment choices?

5. *Choose to talk*. Maybe you're more likely to get quiet than talk when you are in a down mood. Self-absorption is never beneficial, so choose to talk about your mood and why you are in it. Be honest with yourself and with a trusted friend.

When you are in a down mood, why is it difficult to talk to someone about it?

In the situation described above, how might talking about your mood have changed the outcome?

6. *But don't talk too much.* Maybe this seems like a contradiction based on the advice in step 5, but it really isn't. Just as some people are prone to be quiet, others are quick to express their feelings. Use prayer and time with God to determine how much to share and how much to keep to yourself.

In the following list, check the types of statements you might share in expressing how you feel.

- ❍ statements that place blame on someone else
- ❍ statements that are hurting and accusing
- ❍ statements that demonstrate a logic that isn't biblically based
- ❍ statements that build up others
- ❍ statements that point other people to God
- ❍ statements that express your need for God's intervention

Now review the list. The top three responses in the list are not usually beneficial to the situation you are facing. The bottom three are much more helpful. How would statements in the bottom three categories have helped the situation you described earlier?

View "Your Own Pony." What are some things you should pursue?

What are some things you should give up?

Read Psalm 16:1–11. In this psalm, David is expressing his heart to God. There were some things about David's situation that didn't seem fair. He was God's anointed leader, but he was being chased by the ruthless Saul. He had proven himself in battle but couldn't escape Saul's attacks. Life wasn't fair! Have you been there? Look at what David did. He asked God to protect him and admitted that apart from God, nothing he was going through made sense.

Follow David's pattern and express your feelings to God. Admit that your situation doesn't make sense either.

David realized that his focus had to be on God; he couldn't allow himself to be distracted by other things. Can you make the same statement?

David also understood that real joy can be found nowhere except in God. Where are you looking for joy other than God?

Rewrite Psalm 16 as it relates to your life. Return to it regularly for the next week as you focus less on you and more on God.

Take a Moment to Untangle

View "The Holy No." What are some situations in which you need to use a "holy no"?

Be more aware of your moods and the things that affect them. When you see your mood changing from good to bad, ask God to renew his Spirit and to keep you focused on him.

Chapter Eight

Mourning Dew

Our Goal Today: To come to grips with how we deal with loss and discover God's recipe for handling loss his way.

Scripture to Ponder: Judges 16:4–31

View "Your Everything." Describe the last time you experienced a significant loss.

How did you respond to that loss . . .

initially?

after a few hours?

after a few days?

Overall, how would you grade your loss handling?

❍ A

❍ B

❍ C

❍ D

❍ F

Explain your rationale for the grade you assigned.

Loss is a part of life. We can't stop many of the losses we experience. But, as is true in so many situations, we can control how we handle loss. Losses come in a variety of shapes and sizes. It's one thing to lose out on a great deal at your favorite store. It's another thing to suffer the loss of a loved one or the loss of a significant relationship. Sometimes we overreact to small losses and underreact to more significant losses.

How you respond to various situations paints a picture of your emotional state. If you go back and look at the ways you have handled recent events of life, you will see the puzzle begin to come together.

Briefly describe how you deal with . . .

Grief:

Prosperity:

Poverty:

Happiness:

Good news:

Bad news:

Based on what you wrote above, how would you describe your personality?

- ❍ consistent
- ❍ variable

Sorrow is one of the most difficult emotions to handle. Some people shut down; others find it helpful to discover ways to express themselves. Many of our favorite old hymns were written in response to the life experiences of the hymn writer.

If your life could be expressed in the words of a song, what song would you choose or what words would you want included?

Read Judges 16:4–31. Samson's relationship with Delilah was doomed from the start. She was enlisted by the Philistines to discover the secret to his great strength. Three times Samson gave a response to Delilah's request, and three times his response was a lie. Finally, on the fourth attempt, Delilah discovered that Samson's great strength rested in the Nazirite vow he made to God. His hair was an outward expression of his inner commitment. Therefore, if his hair were cut, he would lose his strength, not because of his hair but because he failed to keep his commitment to God.

Think back on your commitment to God. Describe how it affects your everyday life.

What are some things that sometimes overtake your desire to remain fully committed to God?

What can you do to keep your commitment to God at the top of your to-do list? Begin each day with God, asking him to overwhelm you with his peace and love. Flood your day with godly thoughts and words. Listen to God in the music you hear. Meditate on his Word as you move about throughout your day.

Take a Moment to Untangle

View "New Joy." Evaluate the way you handle loss. Let's go back to Samson. What would have happened if Samson had kept his vow to God? How might God have used him for years to come? We'll never know. But we do know that God has a plan for your life. Your life will include things you don't understand and times of loss. Yet God is with you. Continue to remind yourself of his love for you and let him continue to live through you.

Chapter Nine

Breathing Space

Our Goal Today: To discover the benefit of spending time away from routines, relatives, and relationships while still seeking and listening to God's still, small voice.

Scripture to Ponder: Hebrews 13:1–6

Where is your "alone" space?

How often do you get to spend time away from routines, relatives, and relationships?

- ❍ daily
- ❍ weekly
- ❍ monthly
- ❍ quarterly
- ❍ what's time away?

When you have spent time away, what have been the effects in each of the following areas?

Spiritual
Physical
Emotional
Relational

What are some of the ways in which you are encouraged?

View "Unexpected Guests." What is your reputation among those who count on you?

What is the purpose of your friendships?

- ❍ to make me feel better
- ❍ to give me someone to call on
- ❍ to develop a spiritual relationship that helps my friend and me
- ❍ other: ________________________________

Friends provide the following:

Friends help us think. Who are the friends who best help you think? Who are the friends for whom you provide the same service?

How receptive are you to differing opinions on things that matter to you? (Mark the line with an X.)

not receptive |————————————————| totally receptive

Friends help us hear our inconsistencies and pinpoint blind spots. Some people say that we are much more sensitive to the characteristics we share with others. That means that when we are supersensitive to rude people, we might need to investigate the degree to which we are rude to others. Areas like these are called blind spots. Think about your personal growth and list some of the blind spots you have discovered through the years.

How did you discover these blind spots?

What would you do if you needed to make a friend aware of his or her blind spots?

Friends rally when the winds of hardship bluster across our paths. When life gets rocky, to whom do you turn for encouragement?

Who are the people who depend on you for this same type of encouragement?

Friends believe in us. They applaud our gifts and celebrate our good fortune. When good things happen in life, there are certain people at the top of your "people to call" list. How did you develop this type of relationship?

Who are the people who call you when things go well in their lives?

Read Hebrews 13:1–6. In this passage, the author encourages the readers to continue doing the things that had been a part of their faith community. In growing their community of believers, they had entertained strangers. This is something we often struggle to do in our culture. Certainly safety is of the utmost importance, but there are so many people who need to encounter an authentic believer.

What are some things you do to keep yourself in the position to entertain strangers?

Describe a time when you were a stranger and someone entertained you. What has been the long-term effect of that experience?

In entertaining strangers, people put themselves in the position to entertain heavenly beings. This is consistent with the Old Testament examples of Abraham (Genesis 18), Lot (Genesis 19), Gideon (Judges 6), and Manoah (Judges 13). In helping others, we enable God's work to be extended beyond our comprehension.

When we are in need of time alone, we need to understand the promise of Hebrews 13:5–6. God has promised never to leave us alone. That means that our times alone are really times alone with God.

When you spend time alone with God, where are you on the scale below? (Mark the line with an X.)

Talking |————————————————————| Listening

Like the psalmist said in Psalm 118:6, we can boldly claim to be fearless in the face of difficult circumstances because nothing can overcome God's power in our lives.

How does this reality make you feel?

Take a Moment to Untangle

View "Go!" What are some things God has "shouted" in your life? How have you responded?

We should never want to escape life to the point where we are isolated from others. While we need time alone, we need to spend that time in communication with God. That means we should spend time listening as well as speaking to him.

Commit to spending five minutes each day listening to God. Keep track of those things he impresses upon you and the overall effects of your time alone with him.

Chapter Ten

Imagination Station

Our Goal Today: To awaken our senses to God's incredible masterpiece in which we are central figures.

Scripture to Ponder: Colossians 2:1–10

In the space below, list the average number of hours you spend in each activity:

Activity	Daily Hours
time alone with God	
sleeping	
eating, meal preparation, and cleanup	
personal care	
household responsibilities	
driving	
employment	
tending to the needs of family members	
entertainment	
socializing	
reading and/or studying the Bible	
other: ______________________________	
Total ___________	

Based on your total, how many hours do you have available to enjoy God's art or embrace your God-given imagination? ___________

Your response to the question above might be zero! We live in a multi-tasking society that encourages us to cram thirty hours of responsibility into our twenty-four hour day. We're overworked and stressed out. If we ever put on the brakes, we might fall asleep. Somehow we've mastered the art of driving around town with a latte in one hand and the cell phone in the other. No wonder our insurance rates are high!

Reconsider the list of activities above. To the left, rate the priority of each item. Place a 1 by the top priorities, 2 by the second, and 3 by the third. Oh yeah, you only get four items in each category. That means you can't have twelve top priorities. You have to identify the four most important things.

So, what really matters to you?

- ❍ me
- ❍ my family
- ❍ my career
- ❍ my relationship with God

Does the list of priorities accurately reflect your response? If not, why?

We don't get merit badges for being stressed out; we get something else—irritable, cranky, and unhealthy. When you are overworked, how do you usually respond?

Who is most affected by your response?

View "A Pinecone Wreath." What are your hobbies? How much time do you spend "crafting," whatever that might be?

What are the personal benefits of your hobbies?

Have you ever had an experience similar to the one described in the video? If so, describe it.

Even the things we do that don't turn out like we planned have some incredible value. They make us laugh at ourselves . . . much like God must laugh at us!

View "Delicate Snowflakes." Can you relate? Even thinking about such experiences is somehow therapeutic, isn't it?

Read Colossians 2:1–10. Paul said, "Know that I'm on your side, right alongside you. You're not in this alone" (MSG). These were Paul's words to some believers who had never seen him. He wanted them to know that the members of the body of Christ root for each other.

Who is rooting for you?
For whom are you rooting?

In verse 2, Paul identifies the purpose of our fellowship. Read the verse and put Paul's words in your own words.

Notice that Paul wanted believers to be rich, but not in the way that many perceive wealth. How do the riches of our faith compare to the riches of the world?

Be honest . . . which kind of riches are you pursuing in your life?

Take a look at verse 7. The New King James Version uses two phrases that deserve some attention—"rooted and built up" and "established." Review your daily time commitments. Based on your responses, are you being firmly established in your faith? If so, whisper a prayer asking God to reveal more of his plan for your life. If not, what do you plan to do about it?

Finally, in verses 8–10, Paul warned his readers to be careful not to fall for the world's ways of thinking. That danger is still real in the lives of every believer. In what ways are you tempted to embrace the world's ways of thinking?

How effective are you in resisting the temptations?

Take a Moment to Untangle

View "When You Grow Up." What are some things for which people have said you have a talent, gift, or special ability?

Identify three ways God can use the things listed above to give you purpose and to give him glory.

1.
2.
3.

If God put you together for a purpose, he has a place in which he wants to use you. What are some obstacles that keep you from embracing God's special purpose?

❍ fear
❍ doubt
❍ time
❍ money
❍ ego
❍ commitment

Here's a truth that we all need to remember: when God calls you, he equips you to fulfill the task for which you were designed. It is not God's character to call you to a task and then leave you completely in the dark. Relationship with God is your great compass. He will not lead you astray.

What will you do this week to take that next step toward fulfilling God's design for you?

Pray and commit every moment of your life to God for his purposes and see how his plan unfolds. Truly spend adequate time before God with this. Don't rush it. Just rest knowing that God knitted you in the womb, knows every hair on your head and every rubber band in your stomach, and he knows the future he has for you.

Chapter Eleven

Holy Post-Its

Our Goal Today: To fall in love with God's Word and the guidance he provides in its pages.

Scripture to Ponder: Psalm 119

View "The Burning Bush." What are some ways that God communicates with you?

When was the last time God spoke to you? What did he say?

How do you feel when someone doesn't listen to what you're saying?

How do you think God feels when we refuse to listen to what He says to us in his Word?

- ❍ He expects that from us
- ❍ He is disappointed
- ❍ He wants to zap us with a lightning bolt
- ❍ Can we please talk about something else?

We manage in today's world to maintain constant communication. How would you feel if . . .

you had no internet to check e-mail?
you had no cell phone to talk on?
you had no mail delivery?
you never communicated with people you care about?

View "Spontaneous Combustion." In what ways have you waited for someone to rescue you from something you faced? What is the danger of putting your confidence in other people?

It might take awhile, but read Psalm 119. It is arranged alphabetically according to the Hebrew alphabet. It probably is the work of several authors, and it seems to summarize what's needed for a vibrant relationship with God.

One of the main ways God speaks to us today is through his Word. Among its many truths are these six that are of special importance to us as we deal with our emotions.

1. *Live so that you don't have to be ashamed* (v. 6). When you read this verse, you'll see that it is a conditional statement. Read verses 1–5 and list the conditions that lead to a life free of shame.

Are you living this way? If so, how do you do it? If not, how could you live by this verse more fully?

2. *Steer clear of sin* (v. 11). Some sin sneaks up on us because we let down our guards. At other times, we plunge headfirst into sin knowing full well that we are doing something we shouldn't do. In this verse, we see the only way to avoid sin. Read the verse and list what you must do to avoid sin.

As adults, we remember things that matter. Do you remember your bank account number? Best friend's cell phone number? Internet addresses of your circle of friends? Psalm 119:11? Ah, gotcha! Based on what we remember and what we don't remember, we can draw some conclusions about the importance we place on God's Word. What about your ability to recall God's Word when you are faced with difficult choices? Pick out some key verses that encourage and direct you, and commit them to memory.

3. *Look for God to do wondrous things* (v. 18). Wondrous things can be explained only by attributing them to God. We've all seen them. Yet

this verse is based on a request made by the psalmist—open my eyes. This request isn't a once-in-a-lifetime request; it is the result of an ongoing personal relationship.

What are some things you'd like God to show you?

Pray asking him to open your eyes to see the wondrous things he knows will strengthen and delight you.

4. *Let God enlarge your heart* (v. 32). The heart is the center of being in Hebrew thought. This request isn't for a larger blood-pumping organ; it is for God's presence to overwhelm our emotional well-being. Rather than depending on ourselves, we now can turn to God and ask him to step in and take over. How would God's intervention affect your responses to . . .

getting the wrong order at the drive-thru?
encountering a less-than-lovely coworker?
waiting at the doctor's office for several hours for an appointment?

5. *Walk in liberty* (v. 45). The life of faith is a life of freedom, not rules and regulations. God's way of living gives us freedom from sin. It gives us peace in the midst of trial. In what ways have you experienced God's liberty?

6. *Let God comfort you in affliction* (v. 50). Life often is painful. When those times come, we can fall into God's arms and let him comfort us. What better place can we be than in the loving arms of the God who created us? When you face difficulties, what usually is your first reaction?

How might that reaction change if you seek comfort from God?

Take a Moment to Untangle

View "God's Plan." How much of God's plan for you do you understand?

- ❍ none of it
- ❍ some of it
- ❍ most of it
- ❍ all of it

Write a prayer asking God to give you the wisdom you need to seek his plan. Also, list some things God is calling you toward and away from in your life.

Chapter Twelve

Becky's Bangles

Our Goal Today: To discover how God helps us untangle our zany emotions.

Scripture to Ponder: Luke 10:25–28

View "Finally an Author." What are the hurdles you have cleared or need to clear in order for God to mold you into the jewel he desires?

We often are our greatest critics. When challenged with a God-sized task, we list all of the reasons God can't use us. High school dropout, bride at seventeen, mom at twenty, captured by fear . . .

What's your story? We later discover that God can take those things that we think disqualify us and use them to give us unique opportunities for ministry.

What are some things that you might think disqualify you from service to God?

How might God use these experiences to reach other people?

We don't always get to dictate to God how he should handle us. When we do give him instruction, he seldom does it our way. It seems God is better at being God than we are. So, what should we do?

A religious expert once asked, "What must someone do to inherit eternal life?" It wasn't a genuine question but a trap intended to paint Jesus into a corner. If Jesus suggested anything other than the instructions found in Deuteronomy 6:5, he would have been guilty of blaspheming God. If he suggested only the words in Deuteronomy 6:5, people might have concluded that the Jewish way was the only way.

Read Luke 10:25–28. The man's question to Jesus had to do with life after death, but Jesus answered with life-before-death instructions. Jesus' instructions were foundational to the Jewish faith, but Jesus offered a new application. Hope isn't limited to a nation, a denomination, or a socioeconomic group. Hope is a direct result of the following:

Love the Lord. Jesus said, "You shall love the Lord your God with all your heart." We talked about this in the last lesson. The heart is the center of our emotional being. When we love God with our hearts, we let him take charge of our emotions. How will this attitude change your life? Consider a few before-and-after scenarios.

Describe three of your most common emotional experiences. How might you respond if you let your emotions take charge? How would your response change if you let God be in charge?

a.

b.

c.

Care about others. The Bible teaches us to "love our neighbors as ourselves." Loving self is easy. We worry about how we look, what others think, if we have something stuck in our teeth. Then, when life gets testy, we easily mistreat everyone from loved ones to innocent strangers. Jesus said to take the same care and concern you have for yourself and apply it to everyone you encounter. So what will you do when . . .

someone at work makes a mistake that affects you?

someone you love misunderstands something you said?

Work hard. Deuteronomy 6:5 uses the phrase "with all your heart, with all your soul, with all your strength, and with all your mind." This was in reference to the intensity of our love for God. But it applies to every area of life.

How might your hard work affect other people and their concept of what it means to be a Christian?

Laugh a lot. There really isn't a Scripture reference for this, but we know that God has a sense of humor—he left us here! Laughter is good medicine. Not only do we need people around us to make us laugh, we need to be people who make others laugh. We can't go through life taking everything so seriously.

Read Nehemiah 8:10. There is great strength in godly joy. What are the greatest sources of humor in your life? Is the humor God-honoring? If not, you should reevaluate its role in your life.

Never give up. Perseverance is a quality that is rooted in the very being of God. His love for us perseveres in spite of our frequent and repeated failures. If he never gives up, then we should never give up. Too many people live with the dream of getting to stop doing what they've been hating for thirty years. They call it retirement! When we're in love, we don't dream of stopping. When we love God, we don't live for the opportunity not to love him. We persevere in love and in faith.

What are some situations in life that require you to keep on keeping on, even when it's hard?

Take a Moment to Untangle

View "Not the Usual Qualifications." Maybe you don't have degrees, awards, or hobbies that other people have. That's fine—God has a plan to use you. Imagine for a moment that money is no object and you get to do whatever it is that God designed you to do. What would an average day in your life look like?

God doesn't need you to be someone else. He already has people assigned to those tasks. He needs you to do what no one else can do—be you! Pray and thank God for using people like us to deliver his love to a doubting world!

Chapter Thirteen

Emmaus Road

Our Goal Today: To see ourselves the way God sees us and to embrace the marvelous lives he has designed.

Scripture to Ponder: Jeremiah 29:4–14

View "Grow Through Grace." How have you experienced God's grace?

Life is full of situations we wish we didn't have to experience. From lost relationships to lost jobs, from financial insecurities to rebellious children, we are pressed on every side. Even though we don't know what the future holds, we have a God who does know.

Read Jeremiah 29:4–14. Jerusalem had been invaded and some of its inhabitants taken into captivity in Babylon. Others remained behind only to be deported later. From Jerusalem, Jeremiah wrote a letter to those already living in Babylon. In the letter, we see a strategy for dealing with life's problems.

God knows where you are (v. 4). When God sent the people away to captivity, he wasn't surprised when they left! In the midst of our problems, we can be sure that God knows exactly where we are. How does that truth make you feel?

The problem isn't a destination (vv. 5–6). In the midst of the problems, life goes on. We have responsibilities to handle and people who count on us. We can't pull down the shades and have a month-long pity party. Though it might not seem like it, the situation is temporary in light of eternity.

What are some things you've learned through the problems you've faced?

You have something to do (vv. 7–9). Your most powerful witness might come from the midst of the storm. Keep your eyes on God. Don't fall for the wisdom of this world. Don't listen to people who are out of touch with God. Keep pointing people to him even when you don't know what's next.

What opportunities for ministry have your life experiences opened up?

God is faithful (vv. 10–11). God has a plan that is for our ultimate good. He will keep his promises. Though we might desire earthly treasures, God's promise of prosperity has little to do with money and everything to do with a life lived in synch with the Father. We are richest when we are in a right relationship with him.

How has your perspective on life changed because of the life experiences you've had?

God's plan is for spiritual renewal (vv. 12–14). The people of Jerusalem were in captivity because they had been unfaithful to God. After a while, their faith in him would be restored and they would renew their commitments to him.

How have your problems affected your faith?

- ❍ my faith is stronger because:
- ❍ my faith is weaker because:

Take a Moment to Untangle

View "We Need Wind." In what ways have your difficult life experiences made you stronger?

Our problems in life serve to help us strengthen our roots so that we can be strong against future storms and we can become shelter for those who run to us for help. What are three things you can do to become a better shelter for other people?

1.
2.
3.

View "Aim High." As you come to the conclusion of this study, what is God telling you?

In what areas of life will you aim high?